Walleye Fishing Simplified

**Ed Iman &
Lenox Dick**

**Including lake fishing with
Gordon Steinmetz**

Frank
Amato
PUBLICATIONS, INC.

—Dedications—

Ed Iman:
To my parents

Lenox Dick:
To Helene Biddle Dick, my wife, who has edited all my books and given me many ideas over the years.

To Jeanne S. Crawford, who has faithfully typed and punctuated all of my books.

Published in 1999 by:
Frank Amato Publications, Inc.
PO Box 82112
Portland, Oregon 97282
(503) 653-8108

Softbound ISBN: 1-57188-143-3
Softbound UPC: 0-66066-00343-0

All photographs taken by the authors except where noted.
Cover Illustration: Dürten
Book design: Tony Amato

Printed in Singapore

3 5 7 9 10 8 6 4 2

Contents

Introduction   **7**

Chapter I   **Walleye Biology** **8**
Walleye are a schooling, nomadic, contour-oriented predator;
how they bite and eat; family history; winter and pre-spawn period,
spawning period; post-spawning period; summer peak. How
water temperature and barometer affects walleyes.

Chapter II   **Tackle** **13**
Rods, reels, and lines; jigging, bottom walkers, and crankbaits.

Chapter III   **The Properly Equipped Walleye Boat** **17**
Properly equipped walleye boats and discussion on motors and
charts.
   (Figure 3-1) Properly Equipped Walleye Boat p. 18
   (Figure 3-2) Properly Equipped Walleye Boat p. 21

Chapter IV   **Boat Control** **24**
Trolling and back trolling; how to find structures on a chart.
   (Figure 4-1) Back-Trolling p. 25
   (Figure 4-2) S-Curve p. 27
   (Figure 4-3) River Chart p. 28

Chapter V   **Fish Finders** **29**
A must for all walleye fishing; what they can and can't do;
selecting a fish finder.
   (Figure 5-1) Fish Finder p. 30

Chapter VI   **Where to Find Walleyes** **32**
Temperature of water is essential, bright days vs. cold days; what
they eat, basic structures they like; charts, barometer, storms.
   (Figure 6-1) Sample Depth Chart p. 36

Chapter VII   **Baits for Walleye** **40**

Chapter VIII Jig Fishing 42
Types of jigs and how to use them; emphasis on wrist and rod
action; stingers.
(Figure 8-1) Vertical Jigging p. 45
(Figure 8-2) Jigs p. 51 and inside front cover

Chapter IX Bottom Walkers with Spinner Bait 54
Bottom walkers with spinner bait; how, when, and where; bot-
tom walkers can be used with crankbaits as well.
(Figure 9-1) Bottom Walker p. 55
(Figure 9-2) Double-Hook Rig p. 56

Chapter X Crankbaits 59
When and how to use. The puzzle of selecting the correct one;
there are literally thousands of crankbaits with a tremendous
variety of color patterns.
(Figure 10-1) Crankbaits p. 60 and inside back cover
(Figure 10-2) Loop Knot p. 63
(Figure 10-3) Luhr-Speed p. 65
(Figure 10-4) Typical Crankbait Retriever p. 66

Chapter XI Lakes 69
How to fish weeds. When and how to use wind socks (sea
anchors). How to make slip bobbers and when to use them.
(Figure 11-1) Wind Socks p. 91
(Figure 11-2) Slip Bobber Setup p. 97

Chapter XII To Make or Not to Make Lures 98
If you make your own jigs, bottom walkers, and spinner baits,
you an save money and have fun doing it; with advice not to
make your own crankbaits. Ed's secrets not found in any walleye
book, on casting jigs and making bottom walkers, and especially
casting bottom walker leads that are detachable.
(Figure 12-1) Lead Production Pot p. 101

Additional Sources for Reading 106

Introduction

Walleye are one of the more difficult species of fish to catch. An expert walleye fisherman has to have greater knowledge of basic biology and techniques of fishing, than for trout, bass, and steelhead fishermen.

This book is divided into two sections, first for the novice, and second for those anglers who have mastered the basics and desire to go into greater depth and the various advanced methods of fishing. There is one thing Ed Iman and I want to make clear: This book emphasizes the best. By that, we will show you what is the best in rods, reels, lures, and boats. Tackle you make yourself can be the best. Manufacturers do not have a monopoly on the best gear. As you develop expertise, you will be able to cut corners and still fish with the best.

Knowledge is based on the work of previous individuals plus the experiences of the authors.

The following works have been used as background material: Articles from the Canadian Fisheries Journal, American Fisheries Journal, abstracts from the Catalog of Abstracts of the American Fisheries Society's annual meetings, chapter on walleye fishing in McLean's "*Game Fish of North America*," "*Walleye Wisdom*" by Al Linder, et. al., "*Walleye*" by Dick Sturnberg, with at least 100 consultants, including the senior author of this book, Ed Iman, articles from *Field & Stream* and *Outdoor Life*, and finally from the expertise of Ed Iman, a veteran of walleye tournaments, who has fished all over the USA for walleye.

Chapter I

WALLEYE BIOLOGY

Walleye *(Stizostetion vitreum vitreum)*

Originally walleyes were found in a rough triangle through Canada and south to Alabama. Today, because of extensive stocking, they are found in about 32 states and 7 provinces where some have better fishing than others. About 1812, a Jesuit priest stocked the Chemung River, a tributary of the north branch of the Susquehanna River near Elmira, New York, with walleye. The theory of the locals was that he did this to ensure that his parishioners had a ready source of fish for Friday. This was so successful that in a very short time there was excellent fishing for Susquehanna salmon, as the walleyes were called by New York anglers.

The walleye is a schooling, nomadic, contour-oriented predator. Its method of feeding is described as inhaling its prey, and if it is a fish of any size, he inhales it sideways, crushes it in his jaws, and then manages to turn it around and swallow it head-first. Bass, sunfish, and crappie also feed in this manner.

Many fish are described as nibblers: no teeth, poor eyesight, feelers protruding from the front of their heads, and an acute sense of smell. The feelers allow the fish to feel their prey, then nibble it, and in turn swallow it. Catfish and sturgeon are examples.

Dog-biters: These fish have large teeth that bite and tear out chunks from other large fish. Sharks are an example.

Slashers: These fish slash their prey. Trout, steelhead, and salmon are slashers.

The fact that walleyes *inhale* their prey makes feeling the bite difficult. For this reason, rather than still fishing, many anglers prefer trolling with spinner harness and live bait, or trolling crankbaits. The strike is more definitive.

Walleye are slow, determined fighters, but are not comparable as far as fighting ability to trout, steelhead, and salmon. Walleye are more difficult to catch than salmon, trout, and steelhead, but make up for this by being one of the most delicious fish to eat.

Walleye include a European as well as North American species. It is the largest member of the perch family. Closely related cousins of the yellow walleye, as the common walleye are called, are the blue walleye. These are almost extinct. A closer relative is the sauger. When the sauger and yellow walleye hybridize, the result is call saugeye. There is a definite fishery for saugeyes. Walleyes are closely related to the European zander or pike perch.

Walleyes are called by this name because of their marvelous eye structure. A layer in the retina (*tapetum lucidum*) reflects dim light to the rods in the eye. Because of this, walleye see in the dark. Consequently, the best fishing usually is at dawn, dusk, and night. Fishing is usually best during the day when there is a marked overcast. As will be explained later, there are exceptions to this rule. Bright days usually tend to put the walleye down in the deeper water.

Winter and Pre-Spawn Period

50 degrees - 40 degrees F. When fall gradually changes to winter, the water temperature slowly goes down into the 40s. Then the walleye go into the cold winter period. In northern states this means ice fishing. In southern states, as the water becomes colder, the fish become lethargic and a slower presentation must be used, such as jigs. Then as the water starts to warm in the spring, they go into the pre-spawn period.

Spawning Period

40 degree - 52 degrees F. Walleye spawn early in the spring, in water temperature of 40 to 52 degrees F; peak 47-49 F. This is a short period for females, one to three days, and a bit longer for males. During this period, unlike humans, they prefer sex to eating and usually, for a period of about two weeks, they are very difficult to catch, a condition best described as "lockjaw."

Spawning areas usually have a depth of one to six feet. Their eggs require constant aeration. Hence, walleye like to lay the eggs in areas that are shallow and windy. In rivers, they like places with a moderate current and a rocky bottom, where the eggs fall between the rocks, making them safe from egg-eating predators. It has been estimated that 25% of the eggs will hatch on rocky bottoms and 1 to 2% when the eggs are accidentally deposited on soft muddy bottoms. Females do not usually ripen at the same time; hence, some are finished spawning while others have not started. This prolongs the spawning period about two weeks.

Post-Spawning Period

53 degrees - 58 degrees F. The post-spawning period finds water temperatures in the 50s. It takes the fish about two weeks to get their appetites back and become really active. After spawning, the fish disperse from the spawning beds, the females sooner than the males. They all move into deeper water where the temperature is usually the 50s. When the water temperature rises into the 60s, their appetites return. They are now in the pre-summer period and tend to travel in schools of the same size. The larger fish push the smaller ones off the feeding sites. Consequently, you will find large fish together and small fish together. At this time, fish may be at one spot today and gone tomorrow. By some anglers, this period is considered the best for night fishing, and the best time of the year for walleye fishing in general. They can be found in various locations from deep to shallow water. Any basic method of fishing such as jigging, crankbaits, spinner, and live bait can be used.

Summer Peak

65 degrees - 75 degrees F. Early in the season there comes a period which is referred to as summer peak fishing, with water temperatures 65 to about 75 degrees. This is considered the optimum period for catching walleyes, especially trophy size. It is the time of the first hot days of summer, especially the first hot nights. It is also the time when the shallow weed beds grow plankton, and there is marked growth in bottom nymphs and insect-hatching. There are usually lots of fish fry. This, coupled with hungry walleyes, makes for great success in fishing. As the summer goes on, food fish become larger and those trolling crankbaits gradually increase the size of the crankbaits.

As summer progresses the water in deep lakes stratifies into three layers: epilimnion (upper one-third) with warm water 65 to 70 degrees, thermocline, a narrow band of water 45 to 65 degrees, and hypolimnion, a cold bottom layer. The differential between the bottom layer and top layer is so great that walleye go back and forth. Walleye feed mostly in the top layer. When not feeding, depending on the water temperature, they may stay in the upper layer. When the upper layer becomes too warm, they go down to the lower layer. A storm front will push them down into the lower layer.

In rivers the water warms at the top in spring and gradually cools as it descends to the bottom. There is no middle layer. As summer comes on, the walleye will feed in shallow 70 degree water, then go back into deeper, colder water. There is no stratification of warm water in rivers because of the constant flow of the water.

As summer changes to fall and the water gradually cools in rivers, in lakes this is a period of water turnover. The walleye become sluggish and it is then that jigging is particularly effective. The walleye gradually go into the cold weather period.

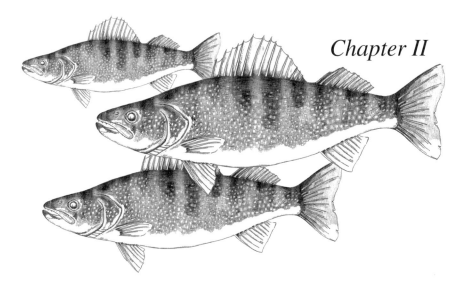

Chapter II

TACKLE

Walleye rods should have a magnum taper, also known as forward taper. This is a rod with the lower two-thirds stiffer than the top one-third. This type of rod has better striking power than the common parabolic taper rods found on some spinning rods and most fly rods. Walleye rods vary in length and strength according to the type of lure weight they are designed to use. The well-equipped angler should have three rods, one for jigging, one for bottom-walkers, and one for trolling crankbaits.

Picking Out Rods

Today most walleye rods are made of high modulous graphite. This material is better for casting than any other. If you are going to pick out a rod from a catalog or tackle shop, you will find a bewildering number varying in price from $30 to $150. Which one to buy? We suggest you start with a rod in the medium-priced range.

THESE ARE THE SPECIFICATIONS FOR ED'S FAVORITES:

Type of Fishing	Handle	Rod Length	Line Weight	Pieces	Lure	Action	Power
Jigging	Trigger	6 feet	8-14 lb.	1	5/8 oz.	Fast	Medium
Bottom-walker	Trigger	6 feet	10-17 lb.	1	1/4 to 3/4 oz.	Fast	Medium
Crank-bait	Straight	8 feet	12-25 lb.	1	1/2 to 1 oz.	Extra fast	Heavy

Figure 2-1

All these rods have a forward or magnum taper. However, as the lure weight becomes heavier, the top third of the taper will become stiffer. Walleye have tough mouths and are gentle biters, so the angler must strike hard to penetrate the bony tissue. Although these rods have specific lure weights, the first two shown in the rod table will handle up to an ounce without harming the rod. However, the heavier the lure weight is than the specified weight recommended, the more difficult it is to hook a walleye. The third rod has a very stiff forward taper. An angler must strike against a long line; hence a long, strong forward sweep of the rod is required.

Jigging

For jigging Ed prefers a spinning reel because it is easier to adjust the line quickly. Many expert walleye fishermen still prefer casting reels. He is vehement in condemning cheap monofilament line that comes on large spools. He uses premier lines.

For jigging with a spinning rod, he recommends Stren EZ cast. It is a soft monofilament line with less memory; hence, there is less coiling.

Bottom Walkers

Level wind reels with Stren Magnum Thin. This is a small diameter, high tensile strength monofilament.

Trolling

Level wind reels for average sized crankbaits, 12 to 14 pound test Magna Thin Line or one of the newer braided lines, which are rated in a combination of pound and diameter, in this case 8 lb. diameter.

When new braided lines came on the market they were thought to be the answer to all line problems. They are very thin and very strong for their diameter, without any stretch when pulled by a heavy fish. Regular monofilament stretches a great deal which can be good and bad. Theoretically, braided line will make a faster and stronger strike. Ed has tested them all and believes braided line should only be used for a standard Crankbait. He feels that the advantage over Magna Stren is only slight.

Spinning and casting reels should be the best you can afford.

Landing nets should be large enough to accommodate fish up to 30 inches. Remember, when possible always land a fish head-first.

Marker Buoys

If your fish-finder has a GPS (Global Positioning System), you will not need a marker buoy. You can come back to the exact location where you hooked the walleye. Tackle shops and catalogs sell marker buoys; if you do not have a GPS, then use a marker buoy. A one-gallon empty plastic bleach or milk bottle with 1/8 inch nylon cord can be used by attaching a 3 pound-weight. I wrap soft wire or string around a rock, then tie about 30 or 40 feet of the nylon cord to it. Next wrap the cord around the bottle. As soon as you hook a walleye, throw the bottle overboard and the rope and weight will unwind. Walleye often are found in schools. When you land your walleye, drive your boat away from the spot and wait for 15 or 20 minutes. Then return and try again.

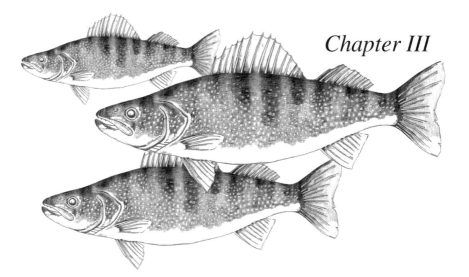

Chapter III

THE PROPERLY EQUIPPED WALLEYE BOAT

❝❝Ed, what is the first piece of equipment an angler should have for walleye fishing?"

"A boat, preferably V-bottomed. That's the best way a person can fish for walleye. It is not nearly as successful to fish for walleye from the bank of a river or lake."

"Okay, Ed. Let's start with the boats. What kind of boat?"

"This depends on where you want to use it. A boat as small as a 12-foot, V-bottomed. This hull design is more stable in wind than flat-bottomed boats. This length boat will do very well if the fisherman watches the weather and does not go much over one-half mile out in a lake, such as one of the Great Lakes. He should have no problems. But if he is a mile or two out in such a lake, and one of those sudden high-wind squalls comes up before reaching shore, he or she may become a fatal statistic. The same holds true for rivers, be it the Columbia in the west or large rivers such as the Susquehanna and Hudson in the east. If a squall comes up, the angler should be able to get to the shore quickly. For a river such as the Columbia five miles below Bonneville Dam, a 14 to 16 foot boat should be safe enough, also on lakes that are about 5 miles in diameter. But on lakes like one of the Great Lakes or on the Columbia River above Bonneville Dam, an 18 to 20 foot boat is barely big enough to venture many miles from shore. Whatever boat the fisherman has, be it 14 to 20 feet, he must use common sense."

I use a 12-foot flat-bottom john boat on the Columbia River. I live about one mile above the I-205 bridge. A boat this size is much easier to pull up on the rocky shore in front of my house. I use it for walleye, shad, bass, and salmon fishing. It is not as seaworthy as a V-bottom boat. Ed does not approve of it. Ed and I have both had long experience on the Columbia, I for 40+ years and he also for a long time. I have sunk two small

The properly equipped walleye boat for the amateur. Outfit courtesy of GI Joe's, Portland, Oregon.

Figure 3-1

drift boats, one on the Washougal River and one in the Sandy River. These accidents occurred in the early years of my boating career. I am alive today because I anticipated these events. I always wear a life preserver whenever I am in a boat. Consequently, I had no problem swimming to shore.

In the Columbia or a large lake, it is a different matter. A life preserver will keep you afloat but will not prevent dangerous hypothermia. Consequently, if you are out in the middle of a large river, you must know the capabilities of your boat. When I am in my john boat with one passenger and the wind comes up and the waves reach about 1 foot in height, I head for shore. I do not stop fishing. I fish close to shore. If the water temperature is in the 50s or 60s, I stay about 150 feet from shore. If it is in the 70s, about 200 or 300 feet from shore. I estimate how far I and my companion can swim safely to shore. For those walleye fishermen who fish in large rivers and lakes with large boats, the skipper must know the capability of his boat and have enough speed to get out of trouble.

Walleye fishing is an expensive sport. However, there are ways an angler can reduce expenses. A boat as elaborate as the properly equipped walleye boat is nice to have. However, this boat will cost a great deal of money. I don't think the walleye care if you do not have the ideal boat. Good second-hand boats can be bought for a third of the price of a new one. The fact that a fisherman can't move rapidly to the bow is an inconvenience, but my old water-ski boat is built that way, and it works well for me. Ed, because he is a professional guide, has to have an ideal boat, but it costs many more times than mine.

"Ed, what material do you like a boat to be made of?"

"As far as I'm concerned, it does not make much difference. Each material has its good and bad points. Wood is quiet and light but needs a lot of upkeep. Fiberglass is heavy and quiet, and needs little upkeep. Aluminum may be the lightest, needs little upkeep, but is noisy if the passengers walk around or drop gear.

"An important item is a compass. If fog rolls in and the boat does not have a compass, any skipper will run in circles until the fog lifts. There are numerous tales of fishermen who have had to spend the night on the water because there was no compass.

"Proper running lights and all the equipment required by the Coast Guard—these usually consist of approved life pre-servers (cushions that act as life preservers are no longer legal), flares, horn, which does not have to be electric. Blowing a simple loud horn is legal. Other mandatory equipment: Standard anchor, sea anchor, anchor lines, and boat bumpers. Rod holders on the side of the boat that allow fishermen not to hold the rods constantly. There should also be rod holders attached to the inside of the boat next to the sides, which allow spare assembled rods and reels to be stored in horizontal posi-tion. Loose rods with reels lying on the bottom are frequently stepped on and broken"

Ed continues: "I do not have a canvas top on my boat. It is almost impossible to fish properly. Some people have canvas tops; when they are fishing they collapse the top against the windshield, and put it back when it rains. I find this is a nui-sance. I like to have my clients suffer a little; it keeps them awake."

"Ed, tell me what you think a boat requires for motors."

"Three or even four motors. First, a main motor, inboard or outboard in the 14 to 20-foot size boat. As I said before, that should have a minimum speed of 35 mph or better. On the transom, a gasoline-powered outboard trolling motor. For a 14 to 16-foot boat, 7 to 10 horsepower. For an 18 to 20-foot boat, 15 to 20 horsepower. This motor is not only a trolling motor, but is also an emergency motor if the main motor fails. This will get you slowly home. The gasoline outboard can be used for trolling and jigging, but an electric motor is another alternative for both of these functions. They are quieter and disturb walleye far less than the gasoline-powered motors. The biggest mistake many anglers make in trying to economize is buying a too-small motor that does not have enough thrust to control the boat properly. Buy the motor that is the biggest you need for your boat, or that you can afford. Watch the classified ads in the paper, and you will find most electric motors for sale are those that are less expensive with a 25 to 30 pound thrust. The owner, after using this motor, realizes that he needs a motor with 45 to 65 pound thrust, and hopes to sell the cheaper motor.

"Most experts prefer the electric trolling motor to be mounted on the bow of the boat, with controls that can be used to steer the boat from the stern. When fishing, a walleye boat is

This is a 16-foot V-bottomed boat, suitable for walleye fishing, with a 25 horsepower outboard which steers from the rear and an electric trolling motor. Boats this size frequently have a 6 to 10 horsepower outboard for trolling and emergency propulsion. A stern-mounted fish-finder and hard metal rod holders are also shown.

Figure 3-2

usually controlled from the stern. Professional walleye fishermen have another electric outboard on the transom for even better boat control. This requires a wider transom than some of the older boats have.

"Batteries must be deep-draw marine type, one for the main engine and one for the electric motor. For the sonar fish-finder, a separate battery is needed. Attaching the cables to a motor battery may produce static in the fish-finder. For the inexpensive fish-finder, lawnmower or snowmobile batteries are fine. Motorcycle batteries probably are as good as lawnmower batteries, except they are long and narrow and need a special holder to keep them upright. The more sophisticated expensive fish-finders need small automobile batteries.

"A sonar fish-finder is as important as a boat for successful fishing. It should be mounted on the transom on the other side of the main large outboard from the smaller trolling outboard.

"The skipper of a walleye fishing boat should be in the stern of the boat for satisfactory boat control. The trolling motor may need an extension steering handle. As noted before, the electric controls for the bow electric outboard are also back in the stern. Ideally, there should be a fish-finder in the bow and the stern.

"The third most important thing to have for walleye fishing is navigational charts. The US Department of Commence, National Oceanographic and Atmospheric Administration has charts of every major river in the USA. Evergreen Pacific Publishing Company, 18002 Fifteenth Avenue Suite B, Seattle, Washington 98155, has taken the large charts for the Columbia River and reduced them in size in an easy-to-use loose-leaf book. There are probably similar loose-leaf books of charts for other rivers. The US Corps of Engineers, each time they dam a river or stream, make a survey of the bottom of the reservoir before they fill it with water; then when the lake is filled, they make a chart of all the various features of the bottom.

There are also excellent privately produced charts of walleye lakes, especially in the midwest. Charts plus a fish-finder will find bottom structure where walleyes like to congregate. How to read navigational charts and coordinate with your fish-finder will be discussed in depth in Chapter V.

Chapter IV

BOAT CONTROL
Back Trolling

T he secret to boat control is back trolling whenever practical. When Ed told me this, I thought as a physician,
"This guy's gone psychotic," but after he explained it to
me, it made sense.

Back trolling is simply having the prevailing wind or current
of the river pushing against the transom of the boat. If you have the
bow of the boat pointed into the wind or current, it will whip back
and forth. Ed explains it in this manner:

When you are operating a boat back trolling, you don't turn
the front of the boat; you turn the back of the boat. You turn the
boat using the motor as the fulcrum. It is like a car with wheels;
when you turn the wheels, the rest of the car follows. In this case,
you turn the motor which pushes the transom one way or the other.
This changes the direction of the bow. Your lines and lures, when
back trolling, are always extended out from the front of the boat.

Back trolling is easier to do with a tiller, rather than sitting up
front in the boat, using a steering wheel, and attempting to turn the

transom. More and more tournament walleye anglers are returning to tillers. Back trolling is done with the motor in reverse. Most motors go slower in reverse, which helps to keep your speed down. Back trolling can be done with the wind or current at your back with the motor in reverse for better control and to slow down speed. In lakes and rivers in strong winds, a lot of power may be needed to maintain control. In this case, some anglers put up splash boards on the transom, to keep the water from coming over the transom. Many anglers won't continue to fish when the wind and the waves are so high against the transom as to need splash boards.

BACK-TROLLING

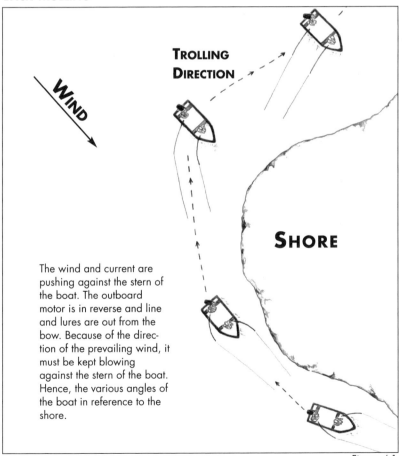

TROLLING DIRECTION

WIND

SHORE

The wind and current are pushing against the stern of the boat. The outboard motor is in reverse and line and lures are out from the bow. Because of the direction of the prevailing wind, it must be kept blowing against the stern of the boat. Hence, the various angles of the boat in reference to the shore.

Figure 4-1

Many people find the concept of back trolling hard to visualize. A typical example of when to start back trolling in a river: You are forward trolling, and your line and lures are behind you. Then the wind picks up or the current in the river becomes faster, and the crankbait or bottom walker is trolling too fast. Simply put your little outboard or electric trolling motor in reverse. Then allow the lines and lures to be out in front of the bow of the boat and continue trolling down stream at the proper speed.

When writing a book or scientific paper, the writer must review the current literature and the knowledge obtained, plus the writer's experience. While Ed has been teaching me, I have also been going out in my own boat and practicing. I have studied elaborate drawings of back trolling techniques. When I am on the water, I find that trying to memorize the techniques illustrated in the drawings is impossible. You have to teach yourself to use a combination of wind and current. At times, the wind or current will not be sufficiently fast and you will use the motor only in bursts to keep your direction. At other times, the wind or current will be such that you constantly have to keep reversing power to slow your boat in a downwind or current. The wind may come from the left or right; you soon learn to compensate. When you compensate, often you will find the bow of the boat pointed directly into the bank as you follow a contour.

Ed states that one of the most important factors in catching walleye is the ability to follow contour lines and recognize structure where walleye like to hangout. On a map contour lines may be actual lines or the equivalent, a series of depth figures. THE BEST WAY TO DO THIS IS BY STEERING THE BOAT IN S-CURVES. Watch the depth on your fish-finder. Example: As you go back and forth, the depth will show 12 feet as you turn right, and then as you turn left, it will abruptly show 20 or 30 feet. Other times it will gradually show 30 feet, as you turn right. Those are contour lines. The farther apart the lines are, the more gradual change in depth. The closer they are, the more abrupt the change in

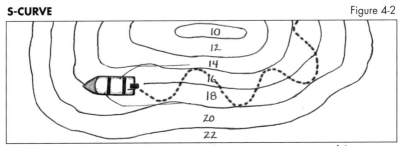

This chart shows how Ed would S-curve in such a way as to cover most of the contours where walleye would be located.

depth. Walleyes like to hang around an abrupt change in depth, especially if the depth change is deep.

Maps of rivers and impoundments produced by the Corps of Engineers show accurate contour lines, sunken islands, reefs, deep holes, and ledges. In the Midwest most maps of natural lakes do not have as accurate structure locations as the Corps of Engineers' maps. Each impoundment or lake is surveyed before being filled. The map illustration 4-2 is of an impoundment behind McNary Dam on the Columbia. is is known as "Lake Umatilla." It is not a true lake; it is an impoundment. It does illustrate all the bottom structures. The fact the beginning walleye fisherman must keep in mind is whether it is a river, impoundment, or true lake, the important structures are the same. The current in the Columbia River in this map is usually about five miles per hour. The big differences between rivers, impoundments, and natural lakes are: Rivers have current; impoundments may or may not have current, while natural lakes usually do not have any current, except if they are small and have a strong stream coming in and going out.

Consequently, after you understand the basic techniques of back trolling, the only way to become proficient is to practice. The nice thing is you can fish while you are practicing.

Anchoring in a strong wind or current, using a bow anchor, will make the boat swing back and forth, thus enabling the angler in the stern to cover more water. In a large enough boat, however, two anglers can fish from the stern.

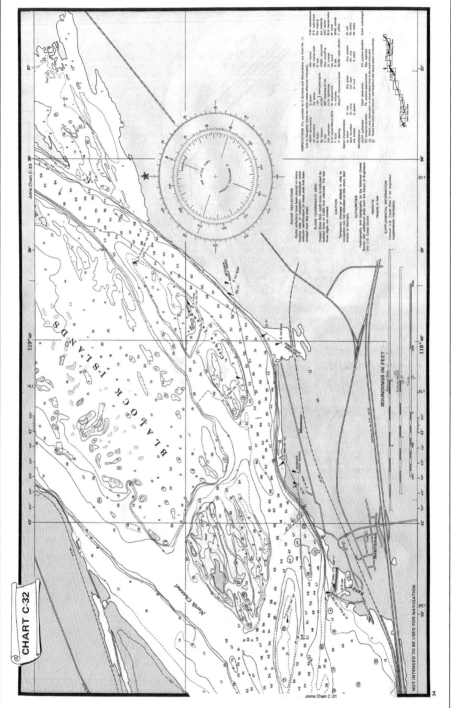

Examine this chart carefully and you will find sunken islands, deep holes, ledges, points of land etc. where walleye lay.

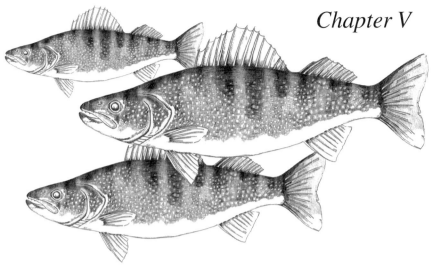

Chapter V

FISH FINDERS

T he main function of a fish-finder is to find the underwater structure where walleyes like to congregate.
Ed says, if you go around looking for walleyes with
a fish-finder, you are wasting 90% of your time. Walleye-
fishing is underwater structure. Once you find a structure
and the machine is in the automatic mode, you may see fish
symbols. They may or may not be fish. In the manual mode,
and if the depth is 20 feet or more, when arches are present
on the screen, they usually mean fish. However, when using
the manual mode above 20 feet, you will often see lines that
are oblique or straight across. The transducer cannot produce arches at this time because it does not see the whole
fish.

To see satisfactory arches, the depth must be 20 feet or
more. At this depth the cone area produced by the transducer
is approximately one-third the depth, or 6 feet in diameter.
At 30 feet, it is about 10 feet in diameter. You can see that

there may be quite a few walleyes around your boat that you cannot see on the screen because of the small diameter of the transducer cone. Above 20 feet you will see partial arches or straight lines. In the automatic mode, the fish symbols that appear on the screen may be just debris and

Figure 5-1

not fish. In lakes, there is usually very little debris, and the fish symbols in the automatic mode are probably fish. A cheap fish-finder in the $100 to $200 bracket is adequate for structure; they should have a grayline feature to show hard or soft bottom. The cheap machines have poor fish arch definition, especially bottom-hugging fish such as walleye or sturgeon. Consequently, expensive fish-finders not only show structure better, but also may pick up bottom-hugging fish. It all depends on the number of pixels. The greater numer of pixels the better definition. Remember, it is nice to see arches on the bottom, but the most important thing again is terrain. Ninety percent of fishermen and many guides just keep their fish-finders in the automatic mode, realizing the fish symbols again on the screen may be debris, especially in rivers. In calm lakes the symbols are usually fish.

What to buy? The cheapest that will show structure or gray line, which tells if the bottom is rocky or soft, and an accurate depth. The most expensive that will show structure and in the manual mode will show the best fish arches.

Professional tournament walleye fishermen all have machines that show arches plus a GPS (global positioning system) which will store up locations where structure that holds walleyes can be returned to at any time.

Some books on walleye fishing spend a great deal of time advertising lures, rods, lines, etc. We decided from the outset that this book's main objective is to teach. We advised beginning walleye fishermen to talk to experienced walleye guides, salesmen, and then make up your mind. Joining a walleye club is a great help. It gives the opportunity to find out what most experienced walleye fishermen use, whether they use the automatic or the manual mode. Don't rush into buying a fishfinder; take your time.

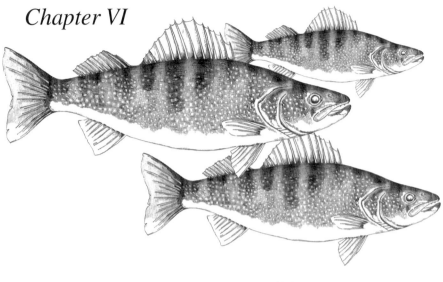

Chapter VI

WHERE TO FIND WALLEYES

"Ed, how can you tell where walleye are going to be located by season?"

"With a thermometer, Len. Remember we discussed how walleye changed location with the definite changes in temperature, season by season. Many anglers seem to forget that a thermometer will tell you by temperature what season is present (See *temperatures for season* in Walleye Biology). Walleye change depths gradually. When you find one walleye at a certain depth, especially during the schooling period, we guides call back and forth: 'Have you got any walleyes, and at what depth?' We help each other. However, in walleye contests where large purses are involved, depth of the fish is a closely guarded secret. It is one of the main reasons that walleye contestants fish the contest areas several days before the competition.

"Other factors are dawn and dusk and cloudy days. Ed says one of the best times to fish for walleye is when there is bright moonlight. This occurs when the moon is half full, until it is full, and continues until the half full moon passes. This provides the proper amount of soft light that makes walleye feed enthusiastically, especially in the fall. Of course, heavy cloud cover will defeat this. Changes in barometric pressure is not as important. All of these factors can produce changes in location. Changes in water temperature produce the biggest changes in location. Many walleye anglers can make a general-ized prediction by consulting their thermometers. One thing I want to emphasize: All I have said so far is true, but unfortu-nately nobody has been able to tell the walleye this, and some-times they are not cooperative. As a general rule though, loca-tion and temperature go hand in hand.

"There is evidence that a rising barometer may make wall-eye go shallower, and deeper when the barometer falls. This is due to pressure changes in the air or swim bladder in the fish."

One of the main things to remember about walleye, they are a schooling, nomadic, contour-oriented, predatory fish. We will use these traits to help us locate walleye. Predatory, they live mainly on small forage fish such as chub, sculpin, bass, perch, etc. Early in spring, prior to hatching of forage fish, they will eat nymphs, leeches, scuds, etc. They are frequently found in schools. Nomadic, they often keep traveling, here one day or many days, and gone the next. The time of year has a great deal to do with where they will be found.

When you first look at a vast amount of water and try to think of walleyes, it is intimidating. Structure is the key to finding them. The basic structure that walleyes like is the same, whether you are fishing rivers, impoundments, small streams, or lakes. They all have most of the same structures, some on a reduced scale.

Contour is not a structure, strictly speaking, but it is just as important. The simplest contour is the bank of a river, stream, or lake, with small projections of land or indentations which, in large bodies of water, become bays and points of land. In the main body of a lake or river are drop-offs that are frequently out from the bank. There may be relatively shallow water, then a drop-off into deep water. This may be a matter of feet or yards. There are sunken islands, reefs, all with contours, and underwater drop-offs. So often when you look at a flat body of water, it is hard to visualize the various sunken reefs and islands, all with drop-offs. In this sunken world, there are many structures such as rocky bottoms with large rocks, sunken stumps, logs, ridges, sudden deep holes, ledges, reefs, and piles of rocks. Sandy bottoms often have ridges which walleye will lie behind. Visible structures are wing dams, pilings, simple poles, bridges, bridge piers, and docks. These are all places where walleye may lie, and they can be found with an expensive fish finder.

What makes structure attract walleye? Food and shelter. In streams and impoundments with current, large rock piles, stumps, piers, sharp points of land, all have cushions of water in front and back. Here forage fish rest and feed on smaller forage such as minnows, leeches, fingerlings, insects, nymphs, etc. Drop-offs are also important. Drop-offs can be small or large. The area just behind a drop-off is where fish like to lie, because water comes over the side of the drop-off creating turbulence, especially when there is wind in the lake.

One of the most important structures are weed beds. Some are found deep in rivers and lakes. I have found weed beds as deep as 20 feet. Weed beds are especially important in the summer when they reach their full growth. Some are sufficiently under the surface that you can pull a simple spinner and worm over the top of them. Others are so high over the surface that they require casting to edges or trolling a simple spinner or worm along the edges. Some anglers even jig with special jigs in the midst of a weed bed.

As one follows a contour with a drop-off, there will also be sunken points of land, indentation of bays, as well as rocks, rock piles, etc. These will often have walleye close by. Many river banks are riprapped with rocks. Walleye love riprap and can be found next to the rocks. Then there are ledges which may be horizontal or vertical. Walleye frequently lie by the sides of these ledges. There are many drop-offs below drop-offs, like a set of stairs; all these may be important areas for fish to lie. When you go to a strange lake, river, or stream, the structures you look for are all the same, with variations in size.

River navigation charts are important to find many of the described contours and structures. Alas, these charts can suddenly be full of errors after high water and especially after a flood, so don't be surprised if your fish-finder can't find some structures where they should be on the chart. Contours shift, as do drop-offs. Sunken islands and most rocky structures usually do not shift. Structures that move, like sunken contours and drop-offs, will be there and can be found with your fish-finder.

One particular formation that walleye like is back eddies. These can be shallow or deep. Walleyes particularly like these because they usually collect all types of food. They are best fished with jigs and are usually good in all seasons of the year. Jigs will be discussed in Chapter IX.

Now that you know the structures that walleye like, next we have to go and find them.

The chapter on walleye biology discussed the various periods of a walleye's life in the course of one year. In the winter time they are in relatively deep water and are sluggish. In northern states and Canadian provinces, this means frozen lakes and ice fishing. In northern lakes such as Wisconsin, ice

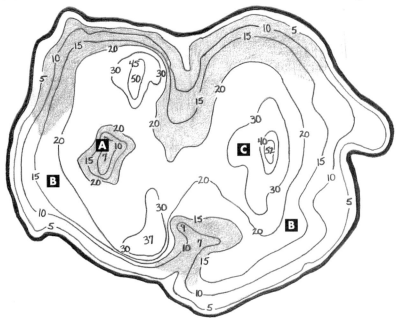

This is a small section of a make-believe chart. At Point A, there is a sunken island. The highest point on the island is 7 feet under water with abrupt contours. The combination of a sunken island with abruptly increasing depth is excellent walleye-holding water. Point B is a sunken area with rather wide contour lines, not a likely place for walleye. The same for Point C, which is a deep hole. The shaded areas are good contours for walleye.

fishing is a popular winter sport with literally hundreds of fishing shacks scattered over large lakes. Some are veritable palaces with holes in the floor to fish through, all the comforts of home including television, etc., while some anglers sit on stools outside in the weather. Fishing is done with bait and tip-ups or jigging. The movie, "Grumpy Old Men", showed many fish shacks.

Ed guides in Oregon and Washington, with frequent trips to Midwest lakes and rivers when they are not frozen.

In states farther south, frozen lakes, rivers, impoundments, and streams are not a problem. The fishing is similar to late fall fishing. Jigs are the most used method of fishing in these states.

Come spring walleyes leave their pre-spawning winter locations and travel to their spawning locations. Walleyes have a strong homing instinct and may travel great distances to their spawning grounds. They frequently use the same spawning beds many times. In northern states they spawn in temperatures in the 40s, while in southern climates in the 50s. Spawning takes place in northern waters in the middle of May, while in the south as early as the middle of March. There is much written about fishing over spawning beds. When they first arrive males and females are hungry. When actual spawning takes place they cease feeding and concentrate. Catching these fish just before they spawn on spawning beds stresses them physically and interferes with successful spawning.

In river impoundments they like to spawn in rocks as big as baseballs to small rocks and gravel. They prefer shallows from one to six feet in depth. In some impoundments the current is so slow that the spawning beds are similar to those found in lakes.

In lakes without any stream inflow they like windy shallow areas near shore and shallow reefs that may be a distance from the shore. In lakes with flowing, shallow, rocky, or gravely inflow streams, these are the locations for spawning beds.

All females do not spawn at the same time, consequently the spawning period may last as long as several weeks. The males hang around the spawning beds for weeks, while females leave almost immediately. One can theorize the longer stay of the males may be to defend the spawning areas against predators. If you know the spawning area, fish the deeper area out from the spawning bed. Here you may catch males and departing females. They move away from the spawning beds and gradually take up summer locations.

This is the time they truly become schooling, nomadic, contour-oriented predator fish. This is the time of feeding frenzy.

Forage fish, although still small, are now a delicious mouthful, and walleye go where they are. Forage fish are apt to be found in relatively shallow, warm water. Walleyes, during warm summer months, spend much of the time in cooler, deeper water. Then they come into the shallows to feed on forage fish in the evenings, at night, and at dawn, and then back into the deeper water during the bright mid-day. If it is a cloudy day, however, they will feed all day long, especially if the barometer is high. There are many walleye fishermen who simply will not fish on cloudy or stormy days with a low barometer.

Ed says this is not always true in a classic statement: "Sure the fishing is more difficult, but walleye still have to eat." Fishing for walleyes in lakes will be discussed in detail in the chapter on lake fishing.

"All that is fine, Ed. But where do I find walleyes from spring to fall?"

Ed laughed, "Go where the feed is."

"How do you locate where the feed is?"

"You can't. At the present time, you have to use the trial and error method. You have to explore all the various structures I have just discussed until you find feeding walleyes. Remember, in the post-spawn period most of the bait fish are gone. All that's left is the large spawning fish that are too large and too active for walleyes to eat, and very small bait fish fry. In the immediate post-spawn time they are feeding on nymphs, crawfish, and other insect life. Later, as the fingerling bait fish grow larger, the walleye feed avariciously on these. This is the reason for using small crankbaits and then increasing the size as time goes by, so that by mid-summer you are using large crankbaits."

"Ed, I have read a lot of walleye literature that states certain structures are better for locating bait fish."

"Len, it just does not work for me. There is one fish-finder that may show forage fish. That is the video fish-finder. It has been around a long time, but never completely perfected. This is a television device and difficult to use. Bright sunlight makes the screen hard to see. In time, when the makers get all the bugs out, these may be the answer.

"Later in the season when some rivers and most lakes have weed beds, this is often where you will find forage fish."

Chapter VII

BAITS FOR WALLEYE

Worms, minnows, and leeches are the common baits used in walleye fishing. Frogs and water dogs are used by a few anglers. It has been estimated that about 75% of all walleyes are caught with live bait. It is Ed's feeling that the reason for this is very simple. The only lures used in walleye fishing that do not have live bait attached are crankbaits. Crankbaits are not used more frequently although best over rocky terrain and they are expensive. In the past 20 or so years, there has been an increasing number of artificial worms and other artificial baits with scents. Many walleye experts claim scented artificial worms are better than natural because they keep the scent longer. Ed does not agree with this concept. He thinks that natural worms are the best. He does advise putting on a fresh worm at least every half hour. Yet the walleye fishermen on the Columbia River universally agree that scent sprayed on crankbaits is essential for their success.

In some lakes toward the end of summer, perch become so numerous that they take the worm off the hook before a walleye has a chance to grab it. When this occurs, Gordon

Steinmetz uses leeches in place of worms. Leeches are tougher than worms, and apparently not as appealing to perch as they are to walleye. In the back of any walleye magazine are addresses of suppliers of leeches which can be satisfactorily mailed to an angler. Leeches as bait are allowed in Oregon and Washington.

Many states prohibit the use of live minnows because of the danger of releasing trash fish in rivers, lakes, and streams.

Keeping worms alive can be a problem. Most of the time the container the worms come in has enough bedding that the worms will stay alive in a refrigerator for three weeks. Longer than that requires a large box with commercial worm bedding with a damp cloth or a damp blanket on the top. It is also difficult to convince your wife that keeping worms in her refrigerator does nothing to the food. Good luck.

In his boat Ed keeps his worms in a commercial Styrofoam worm box about 1-1/2 x 1-1/2, and 1 foot deep, with holes in the top and bottom. A simple one can be made from a small cheap Styrofoam ice chest which are available at most grocery stores. Simply punch holes in the top and bottom. Into the Styrofoam chest, Ed puts ice with no bedding, then worms. The cold of the ice makes the worms lethargic; they absorb water which plumps them up. These worms are easier to handle than those taken immediately out of the bedding they came in. Worms that are kept in their original container get warm as the day progresses and then die.

Minnows, water dogs, and leeches need an aerated-water live well, either portable or in the boat. Frogs are more difficult to keep over a long period of time, and most of the time can only be kept in a wet area overnight.

Gordon Steinmetz, Ed's good friend, has a different method of preserving worms in the boat. This will be covered in his chapter on lake fishing.

Chapter VIII

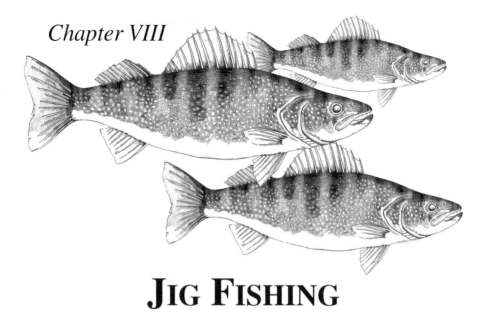

JIG FISHING

❝ ❝ Ed, in this chapter we are going to discuss the three most popular methods of catching walleyes: Jig fishing, bottom walkers with bait, and crankbaits.

Ed, how does an angler determine what lures to use during the various seasons of the year?❞

Ed laughs: "Trial and error. However, to make you happy: post spawn period for about a month to six weeks, jigging; spring until early summer, spinner and worm rigs; late summer to the end of fall, crankbaits; fall to winter, jigs."

Remember, with any method after an hour or two goes by, and no catch, then it is time for a change. Any of the other two methods may work better than jigs in the spring, so it still boils down to trial and error.

A jig is a crude but effective artificial lure made up of a metal head and some form of dressing (see examples shown on inside cover), designed not to imitate a particular food favored by fish, but to attract their attention through its motion in the water. Jigs are the simplest and most ancient of fishing lures.

In fact the oldest known evidence of angling is a carved elkhorn jig mounted on a bone hook found deeply imbedded in a petrified log near the remains of a remarkably well preserved, 14,000-year-old Swiss lake village. Interestingly, next to it were the broken remains of a rough-hewn oak pole and a small woven reed basket, containing the bones of three tiny long-extinct minnows.

This is the first week of October. Ed and I are on the Columbia River, located in the Pacific Northwest. It is the border for a considerable distance between Washington and Oregon. We are near the Washington shore, about three miles above Camas, Washington. The day is overcast with scattered showers.

"Len, there is a basic principle that applies to lures such as jigs, spinners with bait, and crankbaits or plugs. Everything moving in the water produces vibrations. Vibrations produce sound that passes through the water four times faster than in air.

"We are going to start with jigs, but after a period of time if we do not catch any walleyes, then we will change our method to either spinner and worm or crankbaits.

"I know the barometer is down and this causes walleyes to feed less vigorously than on a rising barometer, but they still have to eat. I often have good fishing with a low barometer, especially if it is overcast."

October is a transition period in this part of the country, when summer departs and fall begins. In other states this period may be earlier or later. The water temperature is in transition from warm to cold. This is the time in lakes when the water turns over. When the temperature of the water cools and the surface and bottom temperatures become the same, the wind circulates the water from the surface to the bottom. This is called the "fall turnover." Both in streams and lakes, walleye may seek shallow water to feed. They are, however, not as active. They do not like to move about as much as they do in the late spring and early summer. Hence, in a sense they want their food brought to them.

In this season jig fishing is usually the best technique for fishing walleyes. Some anglers claim jig fishing is the most successful method at any time. Jigging requires more skill on the angler's part than using crankbait (plugs) or spinner bait fishing rigs. In simple terms a jig is a hook with a lead weight on the head. A myriad of artificial dressings may be attached to the hook, which can also be a worm, a minnow, either dead or alive, a leech, or small tree frog. At this moment we are using a round-head jig with a curly-tail plastic grub.

The common method of fishing is vertical jigging, where the jig is given an up and down motion with the line in as vertical a position as possible in the walleye fish zone, which is usually 6 to 18 inches off the bottom. The tip of the rod should be close to the surface with the jig moving up and down in this zone. This is done with a wrist motion which can vary from a slow movement up and down to a snap-jerk.

Wrist action is most important in jigging. When you lower the tip of the rod, you will know the jig is on the bottom when you feel a thunk. Immediately bring your wrist up and then lower the jig until you feel the thunk again. Continue doing this.

(Illustration 2) In this drawing the motor, either outboard or electric, is on the transom, and is in reverse. There is a very slight upstream wind. A factor that must always be kept in mind is the downstream current at the bottom of the stream is sometimes faster or slower than the surface current. This is difficult to predict.

Keeping the jig line straight is most important. The boat must run at the same speed as the bottom current to keep this line straight. In Illustration 6, the jig line is straight and the jig

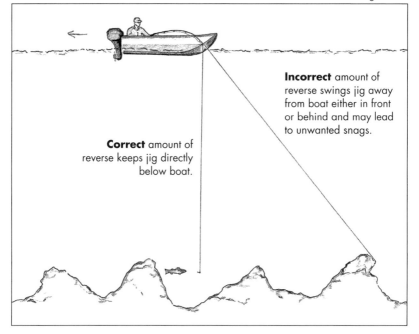

Incorrect amount of reverse swings jig away from boat either in front or behind and may lead to unwanted snags.

Correct amount of reverse keeps jig directly below boat.

is in between the mounds. Then the upstream wind becomes stronger. The drift of the boat slows down, the jig line then goes out in an oblique angle toward the front of the boat, causing the jig to hang up on the mound. The same thing will happen if the boat moves faster than the current. Then the jig will hang up in back of the boat. This all comes under the heading of boat control. You have to be prepared to juggle the speed with either your outboard or your electric motor in order to keep the jig line vertical. In a lake the current is usually a minor problem. There, it is the wind that the angler has to compensate for. In lakes this can be done with wind socks; this topic will be discussed in more detail in the chapter on lake fishing.

Other methods of fishing a jig are: casting from an anchored or drifting boat toward the shore or to a structure such as a bunch of rocks, a piling, etc.

"Ed, I have a problem. I cannot feel the bottom."

Ed replies, "It's tough here because the bottom is soft. When you lower your jig rapidly, you can't feel the "thunk" as it hits the bottom. Under these circumstances, lower your jig slowly and when you feel your jig dragging, which will also make the tip of your rod twitch, you know you are on the bottom. Another thing to remember: the bottom varies in depth, so every two or three minutes feel for the bottom.

"Len, I am going to repeat. Keep the tip close to the surface of the water. The most frequent mistake beginners make is raising the rod tip too high on the upstroke. Then on the way down the line may become slack with no sensation of a "thunk" on the bottom because the line goes slack before you can feel the usual thunk of it hitting the bottom. When the rod tip is close to the water on the down stroke and it goes slack, that represents a walleye sucking it in. When this occurs, strike quickly. Often a bite is a mild sensation of resistance or a gentle tightening of the line, while sometimes there is a sharp pull. With all of these, strike quickly. Once in a while when jigging on a soft bottom, you will see a larger jiggle of the tip that you can't feel; then strike. The walleye bite is the most difficult to tell of any of the fish I have caught. The answer to this is to strike too much, rather than to strike too little. You will often hook a walleye when you don't expect to, using this method.

"The jig we are using at this time is a round-head jig with a plastic grub inserted over the hook and a night-crawler hooked in the middle. Len, this is the jig I use most of the time; sometimes I use bullet jigs and football jigs. As a novice, when you are fishing on your own, use either a bullet jig or a round-head jig. They work about the same. The number of different jigs used under special circumstances is very confusing.

"This jig we are using can be used in 90% of all walleye fishing. True, those specialized jigs may be slightly better for the situation they were designed for. Other jigs I have not mentioned before are the vibrating blade and tail spin jigging spoon. The vibrating blade jig is one of the best methods to jig for walleye. There is one drawback: cost. They are easily lost and are expensive."

"Wow, I hooked one."

Ed: "Put the tip of your rod close to the water."

The walleye comes up but not until it makes one short run. I know enough not to keep turning the reel handle when he makes the run. The drag, which was set by Ed, will tire him out. Many novices keep turning the handle when they have a fish on. Especially when using a spinning reel, it will cause twist knots in your line. When it starts toward you and the line slackens, then is the time to turn the handle to keep the line tight.

The fish is on the surface and I am netting it. One thing to remember: When possible, net a fish head first so it cannot swim out of the net.

"This is a nice fat walleye. He'll taste good."

About 10 minutes later I felt a slight resistance and struck. I pulled up the jig and found half the worm was gone. Ed laughed, "You just had a short strike or, as some say, a short hit. If we have many of these, we will put stingers on our jigs."

A stinger is a short piece of monofilament tied to the hook of the jig, at the end of which is usually a small size 10 or 12 treble hook. The treble hook is imbedded in the worm. Some anglers who feel they are missing strikes on standard jigs, will tie a string with a one to two inch leader to the bend of the hook. With stingers that are used on waterdogs and minnows, the treble hook is imbedded back by the tail. Some anglers use single hooks instead of treble hooks. Most fishermen do not realize the second hook on a spinner and worm rig is actually a stinger.

Stingers with live bait are used in those states that allow live bait. In this case the leader for the stinger is tied to the front of the hook next to the eye, and then the leader is extended to a point a short distance back of the minnow or waterdog's tail. Some anglers claim they spoil the action of live bait, and others swear by them. I use them occasionally with a jig and worm rig such as we are using currently, but this is only when there is a great deal of short biting.

"Ed, are there other reasons why the tip of the rod should be close to the water when jigging?"

"The maximum amount of torque with a good jigging rod is when the rod is in a parabolic configuration. Remember, in jigging, the fish is usually directly under the boat. One characteristic of the walleye is to rapidly swim toward the surface when hooked, with its mouth wide open, shaking its head to loosen the lure. You must quickly raise the rod tip upward so that you can keep up with the rapid swimming of the fish. If you have the tip of the rod at your eye level or above, when you bring the rod up sharply, you will be unable to keep up with the upward swimming of the walleye. You simply run out of lift when the rod tip is way up over your head and that is as far as it can go. Usually the fish will get off if this happens."

Most rod breaks are caused when the rod is held in a perpendicular position, because the maximum pressure is on about the second or third guide down from the tip guide. That is where they break when the angler puts on too much pressure. On the other hand, when the rod is in the parabolic mode, the pressure is equal over the entire length of the rod and it seldom fractures.

"Ed, every time I jig, the jig line, instead of being straight, is angling out behind the boat and I cannot feel the bottom."

Ed turns to me. "We came out on a slack tide; now we have an ebb tide. Remember the Columbia is a tidal river from the mouth up to the Bonneville Dam. This now calls for boat control."

This is the time to use an electric motor or gas trolling motor so we can continue vertical jigging. This same situation occurs on incoming tides. So we will use another jigging method. (I will go into the subject of electric and gas outboards later).

We will use the jig hopping technique. Allow enough line out so that you feel the jig dragging and the line is at an angle of about 45 degrees. Then use a slightly quicker jigging motion with your wrist. This is an excellent way to jig except for one big problem: keeping your jig constantly near the bottom. Again, many jigs are lost with this method.

"Ed, I am beginning to realize why so many anglers cast their own jigs. How much do you save by making your own?"

"About two-thirds the cost of commercial jigs."

"Ed, you mentioned that jigs are best this time of year. What other times are they good?"

"Len, when the very rough bottom structure is such that the bottom-walkers cannot be used, here is where jigs come in handy, especially where there are a jumble of rocks."

We are now back at the dock and have adjourned to a nearby restaurant for coffee and talk about our trip. I especially want to pump Ed for more information about jigs.

"Ed, last night I read the chapter in *Walleye* by Dick Sternberg. It is an excellent book, but like so many fishing books, it is confusing. They show nine different jigs and eight different dressings. Now the jig I am most familiar with is a round-head jig with a chartreuse curly tail dressing and a worm on the hook. If I bought all these jigs and the various weights and all those dressings that Sternberg shows in his book, I would be both crazy and broke."

Ed let out a loud laugh. "There are those who claim anybody

who walleye fishes is crazy, so all I have to do is keep you from going broke. There are four basic jigs which you should have in your tackle box. As a trout fisherman, you know that there are only a few types of flies you really need, although you carry many more, looking for the ultimate killer fly. So it is with walleye fishing. If you stick with the four basic jigs that you need, in four different weights, you will have 90% of the jigs you will need. The four types of jigs are:

"A vertical jig, one that goes straight up and down, such as round-head jigs, which are probably the ones most used.

"Sideways jig, the balance of the jig is sideways and consequently when it goes up and down, it goes in a sideways manner; this type produces a lot of vibration.

"Stand-up jig: This jig, when it lands on the bottom, the hook is above the lead head.

"Spinner jig: There is a spinner behind the lead head in front of the hook. This is a particularly good jig for vibrating.

"Finally, there is a blade jig which is a variation of the sideways jig. There are some professional tournament contenders who only fish with this jig and win many walleye tournaments. One might call it the universal jig. However, the rate of loss is so high you'd better be the first cousin of J.D. Rockefeller. This jig flutters as it goes down vertically. Many amateurs make their own blade jigs. Professionals, however, use manufactured ones because they are more effective than the home-builts. They are fishing in the big money tournaments; consequently, they consider this as part of the cost of doing business."

[Illustration of various jigs - facing page and inside front cover]

"Dressings: There is almost entire agreement that curly-tailed grubs are best. Purchased in bulk they are cheap. The following fluorescent colors should be in your grub selection: chartreuse, universally felt the most effective, followed by red,

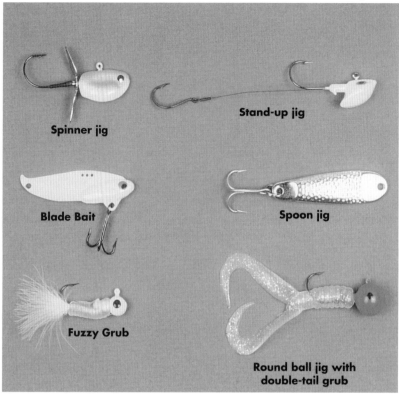

These are only a few of the literally hundreds of jigs available. These will do as a starter. As you fish for walleye, you will acquire your own favorite jigs.

black, green, and white. When you peruse a catalog, you will find multitudes of tints plus a bewildering number of other types of dressings. As you become more knowledgeable you will start experimenting with some of these.

"Weight of jigs: Use the lightest weight that will reach bottom. The deeper you fish, the heavier the weight. On the Columbia River the lightest I use is a 3/8 oz. On quiet lakes I may use an even lighter jig, but for practical purposes 3/8 is the lightest, then 1/2 ounce and 3/4 ounce, occasionally 5/8 ounce. Most of the time the three previously mentioned weights are all you need.

"Generally there is a bait attached to the hook of a jig: A live worm, live minnow (be sure to check local regulations), big leeches, water dogs, and small frogs. No bait is used with blade jigs."

"Ed you have given me a marvelous overview of jigs. I would like you to explain in more detail when to use various jigs."

"As I have told you, the time in the fall when the river water cools and the turnover of water in lakes slows down walleye activity, jigs are sometimes the best method to use. In southern locations in the winter they are good also. They are very successful in ice fishing for walleye."

"What jig do we use then?"

"Again, that's trial and error. As I explained to you, there are four basic jigs to use. Start out with any of the four, then try various colors of curly-tailed grubs. Try a jig with colored head and no body, with a worm on the end of the hook. If you are in a state where live minnows, leeches, and waterdogs are allowed, try them. Also talk to other walleye fishermen about what they are using."

Big fishing catalogs can be bewildering. The number and types of jigs and the prices can be confusing. Dressings are inexpensive. However, a plain jig with hook and unpainted head also is relatively cost-effective. Molds for casting lead-head jigs with hooks included in the case make even cheaper jigs. If you have the time and like to construct lures, these are the cheapest. Most prefer to buy the unfinished jigs and paint the heads, first by dipping into white paint and then the desired color.

The one method of making a jig that can make a real savings is casting and painting blade jigs.

Beware of manufacturer's claims about specialized,

expensive, super-killer jigs. Usually, they are no better than the good old standard ones.

In the back of this book you will find the names of companies that can supply you with molds, hooks, paint, and other supplies to make your own lures.

Chapter IX

BOTTOM WALKERS WITH SPINNER BAIT

As previously discussed walleyes in rivers are most of the time bottom huggers. There are many methods to get a spinner bait rig close to the bottom. To name a few: bottom cruiser, bait walker, needle weight, bait guide, flex-o-sinker, lead cinch dropper with drift sinker, and more besides these. Ed has tried many of these and the only one that has stood the test of time is the bottom walker. These can be purchased commercially for about $1.50, but they are simple to make which saves money.

On the horizontal end of the bottom walker there is a swivel and to the swivel is attached a 12-pound leader, two to six feet in length. Ed's monofilament line is 10 pounds. He uses the six foot leader with a 12-pound test monofilament because it receives the most abrasive abuse. Bottoms with big rocks require a leader of two to three feet. For bottoms with small rocks and clear water or sand, the usual length of the

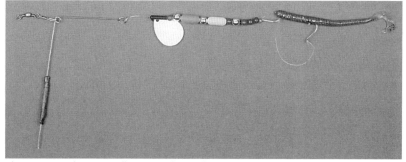

The miniature bottom walker is made small to get it in the picture. The usual bottom walker has a vertical wire of 15 to 18 inches and a horizontal wire, 4 to 5 inches, to which the leader is attached. There is a swivel attached to the loop at the connection of the vertical wire; this in turn is attached to the line.

leader is about six feet to the spinner rig. All the live baits described in Chapter VII: Bait, are used as well as synthetic live bait. To this is tied the spinner rig. Most anglers use worms. Where the law allows, however, live minnows are probably best. Other bait are waterdogs, leeches, and small frogs. Different weights are used on bottom walkers depending on the speed of water flow and depth. In a moderate current, three to four miles an hour and a depth of 15 to 20 feet, a half ounce of lead will suffice. Sometimes as much as four ounces may be necessary to stay on the bottom. You will notice that the illustration shows lead about half way up the vertical wire of the bottom walker. This is the most common place for the lead. Some prefer crimping hollow-core pencil lead to the bottom of the wire. This makes it easier to increase the weight of the lead, rather than change the entire bottom walker.

Now that you understand the bottom walker let's bait the spinner rig and start fishing. The usual spinner rig is first a spinner then a series of different colored beads on top of which is a spinner of various colors; then a double hook, and each hook is approximately three inches apart. Use only big nightcrawler worms. Several little worms on the hook tend to make

DOUBLE-HOOK RIG

Figure 9-2

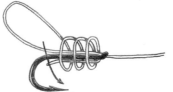

Step 1: Pass 10 inches to a foot of line into the top of the hook eye, lay the line along the shank and form a loop approximately the same length as the hook. Grasp the eye of the hook and wrap the loop over itself around the entire hook.

Step 2: After making 6 to 8 wraps around the hook shank, grasp the line near the bend of the hook at the point where the last wrap was finished. Your wraps will extend from the hook eye down toward the bend.

Step 3: While still holding the last loop firmly against the hook to prevent unraveling, slowly pull the line above the hook until the remaining loop tightens against the wraps.

Step 4: Trim tag against shank.

Step 5: Slide a second hook onto your desired length of leader. Slide a second hook onto the leader and position it above the trailer hook at the desired space.

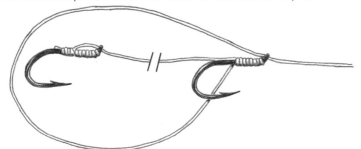

Step 6: Repeat steps 1, 2 and 3. Leave a large enough loop so that the trailer hook can pass through when making the final 6 to 7 wraps. Allow the trailer hook to pass through the loop with each wrap. Be careful not to poke yourself with the trailer as you wrap around the lead hook.

Step 7: While holding the loop tight and the wraps firmly against the shank, slowly draw the loop closed.

the entire rig spin, and walleyes prefer whole, large worms. First put the top hook in the worm's head then the second hook through the dark band about one-third of the way down the worm. You will notice that when you do this the worm bunches and wiggles madly. When you start fishing the worm will stretch out.

Most books that discuss bottom walkers fail to explain how to walk on the bottom with a bottom walker.

You are now seated in the back of the boat and have let out 20 or 30 feet of line, and you feel the bottom walker touch the bottom. Now is when the technique of walking a bottom begins. As soon as you feel the bottom flex your wrist up and pull it off the bottom. Immediately flex it down until you feel it touch bottom again, then instantly flex your wrist up and bring it up. If you find that the sinker on the bottom of the bottom walker is dragging, then shorten the line. If you allow it to drag it will quickly hang up. If you find it is not touching bottom then lengthen the line. At times you will have to either add a heavier or lighter weight.

One of the big problems with bottom walkers is tangles. If you toss it in, it will invariably tangle. Let it in slowly, watching all the time for tangles. The deeper the water the heavier the weight that must be used. A simpler method of using a bottom walker is to obtain the wire part of the bottom walker alone and use changeable weights. It is much faster to change weights rather than replace the entire walker. Interchangeable weights can be purchased or you can make your own. The homemade ones require a simple kink in the wire to hold the weight up. Bottom walker weights vary from one-half to four ounces, depending on conditions.

When walking a bottom walker over a hard rocky bottom it is easy to feel the bottom. A sandy bottom is much more difficult to fish; be sure you let out line slowly. You may not be able to feel this bottom. Watch the tip of your rod; when it jiggles, you are on the bottom. The same wrist action is used as on hard bottoms. Consequently, every time the tip jiggles, go up with your wrist and then down. Hard rocky bottoms require a more pronounced jerky action to keep the bottom walker from hanging up.

In place of a spinner bait rig a floating crankbait can be substituted and the same techniques of walking the bottom walker across the bottom apply.

Hooking a walleye: A walleye bite is much different than that of a trout, steelhead, or bass. Most of the time a walleye bite is a sense of resistance or occasionally a click sensation. At times it can be a definitive tug. Any of these sensations means a quick sharp pull with a rod. Later you will learn to give a little line before you strike. At this stage in your walleye angling career, strike when you feel anything different. It is better to strike frequently than not strike enough. You will be surprised how frequently you will hook a walleye by using this technique. As you mature in your fishing skills you will learn what is a real bite and you won't have to do so much striking.

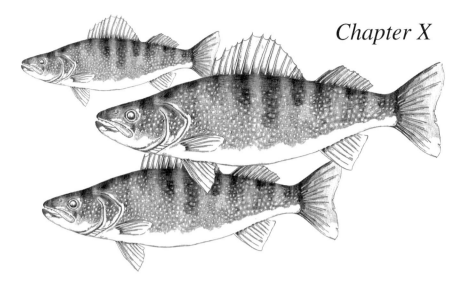

Chapter X

CRANKBAITS

There is a great deal of confusion as to which is a crankbait and which is a plug. Some call everything crankbaits and then divide them into long narrow minnow plugs and stockier-shaped minnow plugs. Ed thinks this classification is nonsense and prefers to call all of them crankbaits: Long slender minnow crankbaits used for trolling and short stockier ones for casting. The short stockier ones have a more pronounced wobble in the water and are fished with more speed than the minnow type which have a much narrower wobble. Depending on the length of the bill, all of these may be shallow, medium depth, or deep-diving. Some crankbaits have neutral buoyancy.

As we stated in the beginning of this book there is a list of books that we feel will help to increase your expertise as you become more experienced in walleye fishing. There is one book, however, that every walleye angler should have from the beginning: *Crankbaits* by Mike McClelland,

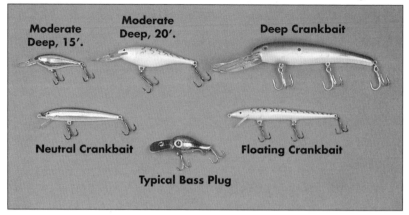

Moderate Deep, 15'.

Moderate Deep, 20'.

Deep Crankbait

Neutral Crankbait

Floating Crankbait

Typical Bass Plug

Fishing Enterprise Press, Box 7108, Pierre, South Dakota, 57501.

Many crankbaits have the depth they should reach marked S-20 or S-30, meaning 20 or 30 feet depth, which is the depth the particular crankbait is supposed to reach. *Crankbaits* contains pictures of every crankbait made by the manufacturers, with tables showing trolling depth for size of crankbait, optimum speed that should be used for trolling and for cast. I use the information in this book constantly and would not be without it.

The neutral buoyant and floating types of crankbait have the same profile as the deep-divers but with a short bill. These are used with bottom-walkers. They usually come in different sizes and colors. In trout fishing the angler attempts to match the hatch. In walleye fishing there is an attempt to imitate the forage fish they prey on, such as shad, chub, sunfish, perch, sculpin, crawdads, etc. Consequently, in the spring many anglers use small crankbaits and as the season progresses, larger crankbaits. Commercial crankbaits include the following colors: gold crawdad, clown, shad, fire tiger, silver-blue, orange crawdad, silver-chartreuse, and rainbow perch. Ed particularly likes the following combination of colors: yellow and chartreuse, chartreuse and orange, white and chrome with blue back, imitation shad, and small minnow. This is where discussion with local anglers is helpful as to which colors are best at what time.

However, many experts contend that the color is less important than the wobble. They claim that one crankbait will excite and hook more walleyes than a seemingly identical one simply because it has a different wobble. When you have one of these wonder baits, keep it in a safe!

We are now in the boat. The depth of the water is about 20 feet. We are using 12-pound monofilament line. How can we tell how much line to let out? One of my favorite methods is to stretch out the line prior to going fishing and then with a black indelible felt pen at 100 feet make a three-inch long mark, and then a second mark at 25 feet. The mark is best seen when it comes up into the reel. As it winds in, the three-inch mark shows very visibly.

Recently I have gone back to a method I used in the past when trolling for salmon—line pulls. Take the end of the line in your right hand, put the reel in the middle of your abdomen, extend your arm straight out. My reel to straight right arm is three feet. In my case, each pull is three feet. When I pull 34 times, I have extended the line 102 feet.

The above methods of measuring line when trolling crankbaits work but they both have drawbacks: Line pulls are cumbersome and slow. Every time you bring your crankbait in you must again pull off 35 armlengths to reach 105 feet of line. The use of indelible ink at a measured 100 feet works well. But, alas, the ink washes off in about six to eight hours of use. Guides do not use either of the above. From long experience they can sense when the line is out 100 feet or more.

I live on the Columbia River and keep a 12-foot john-boat with a six horsepower outboard pulled up on the beach. Consequently, I am able to practice the various walleye fishing techniques that Ed has taught me. One day while I was trolling with a crankbait I suddenly had an idea: Why not use a slip bobber knot to mark 75, 100, and 125 feet? (See Chapter XII, page 97) This knot is easy to tie into the line, will not slip, and goes into the reel arbor with no difficulty. So far it has worked very well for me.

There are four major factors which determine the depth a crankbait will run in addition to the size of the bill. The bigger the bill, the deeper the crankbait will run. Other factors are line diameter, length of line, and the fourth factor is boat speed. Our goal is to keep the crankbait in the bottom two feet of the river or impoundment. The walleye are usually found here. This is frequently referred to as the fishing zone.

Before you start fishing any crankbait you must be sure it is properly connected to your line. Some use a loop knot or a split ring. Do not use a swivel. The loop knot is done the same way as it is for the crankbait, with a short line behind your boat. Be sure it tracks in a straight line. If the lure tends to run to the left, turn the eyelet to the left and vice versa. One other bugaboo is proper speed to pull the crankbait. Let out as much line as you can while still seeing the crankbait. Then increase the boat speed until it starts to twist. Slow down until you estimate there is the most pronounced wobble. This is considered by some the proper speed to drive your boat.

We will now tie on a diving crankbait that theoretically goes down to 20 feet. We are going to troll upstream. At this time we will determine boat speed by trial and error. We keep the boat speed a little faster than the current, whether

LOOP KNOT Figure 10-2

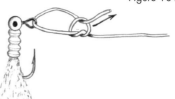

Step 1: Tie an overhand knot 6 inches from the tag end. Leave overhand knot loop slightly open. Pass the tag end through the lure/eye, leaving 1 inch between eye and loop.

Step 2: Run the tag end back through the loop as shown.

Step 3: Make 3 to 4 wraps around the standing line.

Step 4: After completing the wraps, run the tag end back down through the overhand knot loop, then . . .

Step 5: . . . back through the larger loop. Steadily pull on the tag end and the standing line simultaneously, being careful not to allow the wraps to bunch up.

Step 6: Trim.

fishing up or downstream. We depend on the best lure vibration to ascertain the correct speed. This will work but there is a better method which will be explained later in this chapter.

Diving crankbaits are usually trolled upstream, while floating crankbaits, attached to a bottom-walker, are used in either direction, similar to the method used for spinner rigs and worms. We have let out 75 feet of line slowly. You can feel the lure vibrating, but as yet do not feel the bottom. Most crankbaits often take minutes to reach bottom, which is why we let out the line slowly. Crankbaits reach their maximum depth at about 100 to 120 feet. Now you can feel the lure touching the bottom, and if you are lucky will still feel the vibration of the crankbait, although crankbaits may be vibrating and the angler not realize it. Novices frequently let out too much line too fast; as it goes out there is a certain distance where they are unable to feel the lure vibrating. Also, with too much line out, there are frequent hang-ups. As you troll the crankbait frequently give the line a couple of jerks with your rod. This can entice the walleye to strike.

Again, one of the most important factors in trolling a crankbait is speed. MOST BEGINNERS TROLL TOO FAST, myself included. Many times I have been trolling a crankbait. The next thing I know, the crankbait, instead of being at the depth I want it, the miserable thing is on the surface. When this happened, I reported to Ed, and he laughed.

"There is nothing wrong with the crankbait. It is you. You are pulling it too fast. Remember—I told you a little faster than the current."

"Well, Ed, how do I tell how fast the current is? It's fine for you because you have been doing this for a long time. You can look at the current and the crankbait and tell how fast to pull it. As you have told me many times different crankbaits have different speeds for optimum action."

"Len, I guess you're right. For speed, look at the speed your boat is going and then the amount recommended. You can find this in Mike McLelland's book. Various crankbait speeds average from two to four miles per hour."

That's fine except inexpensive fish finders do not have speed indicators on them. What now to do? Ed and I both agreed to use brand names as little as possible. One day when I was shopping at a local tackle shop, I spied an inexpensive

speedometer that an angler can hang on the side of the boat, Luhr-Speed, manufactured by the Luhr-Jensen Company. They claim it is very accurate. For the angler with an inexpensive fish finder it should be the answer to speed problem. Some guides use both their fish finder and this device. I have found it a tremendous help.

One problem all walleye fishermen sometimes face: You can't get the crankbait down to the bottom. The answer is to gradually put small amounts of lead weights 18 inches above the lure.

Now our fish finder is important. You must watch the bottom for obstructions such as ridges, outcroppings, drop-offs, stumps, rocks, etc. When these appear reel up and at the same time lift the rod tip. Unfortunately, this does not always work and then the crankbait is stuck. When this happens I turn the boat around downstream until the line tightens. Then I give a jerk. If this does not work, drive the boat up until the line is

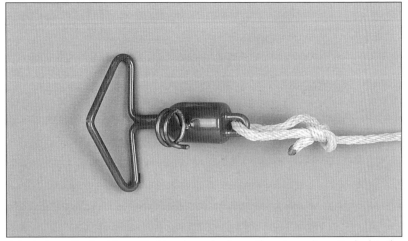

A typical crankbait retriever. It slides down the line with a strong line attached to the retriever, which is used to dislodge and pull the crankbait up to the boat. This is a must with all crankbaits.

straight down. Then use a lure knocker attached to some light but strong nylon line to release the lure. This will save a lot of crankbaits. Alas, there are a great many that don't come loose. One expert tournament walleye angler stated that when fishing with a trolled crankbait it is common to lose a dozen in a day!

Good, you have hooked a walleye. Now the fun begins. Take your time bringing it in. They usually do not take long to net. Big walleyes, however, so-called trophy size, will take much longer to land.

Now, that the fish is landed, Ed will tell you more boat handling.

"There is one very important thing that I have been doing while you were fishing. That is, S-turns. I drive the boat gradually to the left until the depth finder tells me that the depth is about 12 feet; then I turn right gradually until the depth finder shows about 25 feet. In doing this, I am following the contour line. This is why I tell you to reel up about five or 10 feet, and then when we go into deeper water, let out five or 10 feet.

During this time, you occasionally have to let out enough line to again feel the bottom. If we catch a fish at 15 feet, I will then straighten out the boat and troll this depth in hopes that this is the level where we will find more walleye. Many anglers toss out a marking buoy where a fish is caught because many times other walleye will be in this location. Now we will turn around and go downstream. We will use the same bottom walker we used with the spinner rig, only we will use a floating crankbait with the usual short bill.

The area we have been trolling over is rocky and either the deep-diver crankbait technique, or the bottom walker and floating line will work. There is terrain where the bottom walker technique will work better. Sandy bottoms: The deep diver lures kick up more sand as they go along the bottom. Ed feels this goes into the walleye's gills and drives them off, while the bottom-walker kicks up very little sand. The fish seem to prefer bottom-walker technique in this instance. Deep divers, however, seem to work better on gravel and rocky bottoms with drop-offs.

Another reason to change from one technique to the other: The deep-diver has a very definite wobble action, while the bottom walker with a floating lure has a more swimming action. Consequently, after using a deep diver crankbait for an hour or so and nothing happens, change to a bottom walker and floating crankbait or vice versa. This often will provide a strike. With the bottom-walker technique on sand, you use a six or eight foot leader. When using it on rocky bottoms, you shorten the leader to two to four feet. The shorter leader has less hang-up.

Another factor to be considered is the sharpness of the hooks. Most crankbaits come with sharpened hooks but not always. Some need touching up with a hook file. Others need replacing with better hooks, such as a Gamakatsu with a round bend and a straight point.

An interesting and sometimes very effective method is to take a neutral or floating crankbait, remove all the hooks, then tie on a four to six foot leader to the front screweye, then to the end of the leader tie on a spinner worm harness. The crankbait will carry the spinner worm harness to the bottom and allow it to work along the bottom. The wobbling of the crankbait adds to the action of the spinner worm harness.

It's getting late. Let's go to the dock.

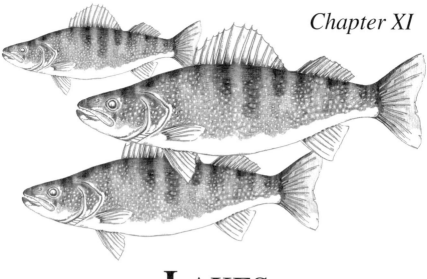

Chapter XI

LAKES

Lakes throughout the USA and Canada historically contain about 90% of all walleyes, rivers about 10%. However, the increased number of rivers with impoundments that did not originally have walleye populations, such as the Columbia River in Oregon and Washington, the impoundments in the Missouri system, the TVA impoundments in Tennessee and Kentucky, and others, have probably changed the percentage to 60% lakes and 40% rivers and impoundments.

Many books classify walleye lakes in three categories with fancy scientific terminology.
Eutrophic - Good fertility
Mesotrophic - Middle fertility
Oligotrophic - Poor fertility

Most natural lakes were made by the action of glaciers during the ice age. Many oligotrophic lakes are found in northern

Montana, northern parts of North Dakota, and Wisconsin. The rest of the USA is either eutrophic or mesotropic. There are differences in the water characteristics between eutrophic and mesotrophic lakes. From the practical point you fish both types the same way. Eutrophic lakes are apt to have more weeds and other plants, while mesotrophic lakes have less weeds and plants.

It takes a long time to learn how to judge the fishing in various lakes, rivers, impoundments, and streams. The most practical way to find out this information is to contact the game and fish commission of the state where you wish to fish. There are 32 states and 7 Canadian provinces that have walleye. You can obtain a list of the state game commissions from your local library.

We did this and the results were astounding. For approximately $10 postage, we received masses of information. This is obviously done to encourage tourism which provides a great deal of money for various states. Many of the brochures were so large that the postage was $3 or $4. Most told you the counties with the lakes, rivers, and impoundments where the best walleye fishing is located. They encourage you to call regional offices located throughout the state. A call to one of these offices will give you more information about the best fishing, plus current conditions and catch. The brochures and pamphlets frequently have detailed maps and a great deal of how to fish for walleyes, as well as for many other species of fish. The maps were mostly for lakes and impoundments. They did not show the underwater topography. However, most large lakes have maps with this information that can be obtained from local tackle shops.

We have not discussed the water turnover of lakes. This is important to know. It has a great bearing on where you find walleye in different seasons. In the spring when the surface water gradually warms and summer develops, the water in relatively deep lakes stratifies into definite temperature levels. Partially due to wind action, as the water warms at the surface, the cold water sinks to the bottom. There develops a band of rapid temperature change, known as the thermocline. As fall develops and the temperature of the air gradually becomes colder, with the added effect of fall wind and rain, the surface of the water becomes cold and sinks down. It comes in contact with the deeper water which, though cold, is warmer now than the surface water. The narrow thermocline breaks up and the bottom water turns over and becomes the top. The lake now has approximately the same temperature as the bottom. This can be quite violent, and in some lakes the stagnant bottom water may even smell, and dead weeds and other bottom debris may appear on the surface. Some lakes are so shallow that the above sequence does not occur. In rivers there is no turnover. In summer, the surface water is warmer than the bottom water.

Having thus set the stage, lets go back to spring. The same phenomenon of periods develop, pre-spawn, spawn, post-spawn, as spring gradually turns to summer.

Walleye in lakes like the same types of gravel, rocks, etc. that the river walleye do. If there is a feeder stream into the lake and proper terrain, they will spawn there. They will also spawn in the shallow rocky gravel on the prevailing windward side of the lake, where the water will be circulated by the wind. Walleye eggs require a certain amount of water flow to be viable. The walleye often spawn on shallow reefs in lakes.

The walleye then go through all the periods of a summer, fall, and winter that river walleye go through.

It is necessary to be able to recognize lakes that go from very fertile to less than optimum. High fertility lakes: these lakes have large quantities of submerged weeds. In the summer they shelter small fish and insects. The shade that is provided is the reason that walleye will rest in the dense part of the weed bed. When they are in this location they are difficult to catch. Walleye migrate back and forth from the deepest part of the lake that is above hypolimnion. Below the hypolimnion on deep lakes there is usually not enough oxygen to support life. Consequently they do not venture any deeper. Poor fertility lakes are usually shallower than good fertility lakes. Because of the shallowness of these lakes, there is more penetration with sunlight and the walleyes do most of their feeding at night.

Where to Find Walleyes in Lakes

The first thing to remember about lakes is that the structures that walleye like in rivers are the same in lakes. There are few differences. Rivers, as a rule, do not have as many weed beds, but in shallow bays where there is calm water they will have weed beds in the summer. This is particularly true of impoundments with shallow bays and weed beds. At times some impoundments may have such a slow current that for practical purposes, they are lakes.

After spawning the female walleye move out from the shallow spawning beds near shore and from spawning beds on reefs to deeper water. As in rivers the males hang around the beds for prolonged periods before they too migrate from the beds. They then move out in the lake and become contour-oriented. They are frequently found on the edges of weed beds, points of land, sunken reefs, and islands with drop-offs, similar to those in rivers. They come out of the deep water to feed at dusk, during the night, and remain till dawn gives way to morning when they return to deep, cooler water. The same phenomenon of cloudy days will find them feeding. They cease feeding liberally when a cold front passes through and for a day or two afterward. But, as Ed says, they have to eat, and good fishing occurs.

More About Lake Fishing with Gordon Steinmetz

"Ed, we have spent a great deal of time discussing lake fishing. We agreed we would go to a lake sometime in May."

"Len, I know I agreed. I can't do it. I am too busy guiding at this moment. I have a good friend, Gordon Steinmetz. He lives on Banks Lake in Washington State. His tackle shop and restaurant are about one mile from Coulee City, Washington, and about thirty miles south of Grand Coulee Dam. He guides Banks Lake and other walleye lakes. He will be down here in June to enter the lower Columbia River walleye tournament. Like me, he can guide on both rivers and lakes. His home base is on Banks Lake, while mine is the Columbia River."

I made an appointment with Gordon to guide an old fly fishing friend, John Bassett, a retired general surgeon, and me on Banks Lake. Banks Lake is 300 miles from the Vancouver, Washington/ Portland, Oregon area. Banks Lake is an artificial lake made by pumping water from the Grand Coulee into the lake. It is 30 miles long. Its outlet is at the southern end of the lake. The water is used to irrigate a tremendous area of northern Washington. It is a true artificial lake, not a river impoundment. The surrounding country is some of the most beautiful I have ever seen. There is a wide canyon, about one to two miles wide, with numerous natural lakes, as well as Banks Lake, including Grand Coulee Dam with Roosevelt Lake behind the dam.

When I go fishing with Ed he gives me hands-on experience so I can describe the physical methods of walleye fishing. I soon realized, as did Ed, that I could not take notes and fish at the same time. Consequently, after each boat trip I would go to his house, or he to mine, and we would go over the previous trip with the tape recorder running. Then after he left I would write up the previous boat trip. I knew that same thing would occur when I went fishing with Gordon Steinmetz.

I made a date with Gordon to go fishing on Banks Lake. At the time I made the date, I asked him if he would mind tape recording his instructions at a later time. He laughed and agreed.

We met Gordon at the boat landing at Banks Lake at our appointed time. Gordon Steinmetz has the same stocky build as Ed Iman. Like Ed, he is in his middle 50s with graying hair. While we were transferring gear, lunch, rain coats, etc., into his boat, he told us about the lake.

Banks Lake varies in width from one-quarter mile to three miles. Much of it is about a mile wide. There is every type of terrain that can be found in any lake, with the exception of those lakes with inflow or outflow streams. There are islands, points of land, both above and below water, shallows with weeds, bays, both shallow and deep, and many underwater drop-offs, and rip-rap banks.

Gordon's boat is 20 feet long with the same configuration and equipment as Ed's, including a fish finder in the bow. There are two other pieces of equipment that Gordon has on his boat that Ed does not: several sea anchors or drift socks, varying from small to quite large, and splash guards on the stern of the boat for back trolling.

After we had left the landing and traveled a short distance, Gordon stopped the boat. "We are now in the immediate post-spawn period. The fishing is good but will be better in another month."

From then on I decided to wait until Gordon was on dry land and I could tape his fine discussion on lake walleye fishing.

"What we are going to try to do is keep this as simple as we can. We are not going to fill everybody full of a bunch of gobbledy-goop and this type of thing. The first thing we have to understand about walleyes is they don't make decisions. Walleyes are going to eat. I don't care if you are in Coulee City, New York, or South Dakota. A walleye is a walleye. The first thing we have to do is to keep it simple. I don't care if you're in a reservoir or in the Columbia River, a walleye is going to do the same thing. He is going to eat. The first thing you have to realize about a walleye, he is not a slasher, he is not a dasher, he is not going to go out and bust up a bunch of game fish or bait fish, or this type of thing. He is going to be an opportunist. He is going to sidle up to it, very gently; he is not going to expend a lot of energy. He is going to open his mouth, flare his gills, and suck in a volume of water. A bait fish is buoyant, so all a bait fish does is go with the flow of the water, and when he sucks in that water, he sucks in the bait with it. He doesn't run out and dash and this type of thing.

"Another thing you want to realize about walleyes is, they don't make a decision. The fisherman makes the decision about where he is going to fish. There are millions and millions of articles out there on walleyes, and there are a lot of articles out there to sell tackle. I'll tell you right up front that's all they're for. You can separate the myths of advertising and this type of thing from fishing and good products. There are products that will catch fish; there are products that the only reason they are out there is to sell products. You can go out there with a jig, no color on it, a bare hook and a little piece of worm or a leech or something like that, and be just as successful.

"In spring of the year is when we start using jigs up here. First the ice goes off; in a lot of the reservoirs out here we don't do a lot of ice fishing for walleyes in the Northwest. I have been asked that 1000 times. In Banks Lake, I have probably drilled 10,000 holes trying to catch them, and its just one of those things. A deeper lake, 80 feet deep, and the bait fish seem to go deeper with them–Yeah, there's an occasional walleye caught up shallow, but we have had no success out here whatsoever ice fishing for walleyes. There have been some caught, don't get me wrong; there have been some, but we are not going to get into that too much right now.

"What we are going to talk about is the spring of the year. The walleye warms; they go through their hormonal deal. They are going to eat. They are going to spawn, and they are going to eat some more, and its just the cycle that they go through. The first thing you can do when you go to a lake that you're not familiar with is don't just throw your boat in the water and take off. Go talk to somebody, talk to a tackle shop, somebody that is in the business, somebody that walleye fishes. Talk to other fishermen. Go down to the dock. Most fishermen, if you're friendly with them, they are going to be friendly with you. One thing I have found out about walleye fishermen, they will share their information. There might be some times in tournaments when they are not going to share everything with you, but they are not going to turn their backs and just snub you like a lot of fishermen would.

"Get yourself a map if you can't find any other information. Drive up the lake, look at it. Look at the structure. Put some thought into what you are going to do before you go out there. We talk a lot about, Boy, we're jigging or whatever we are doing, we are getting short bites. You see them with spinners, you see them with crankbaits, you see them with jigs. You come into the dock and say, Man, they were really short biting today. We went through five dozen crawlers or whatever and all I got was half a crawler back. I'll tell you something, that walleye doesn't make a decision to swim up there and say,

Wow, there's a nightcrawler with a hook in it. I think what I am going to do is swim up there and just bite the last half of the crawler off. He's not thinking; he's trying to bite the worm, that's what he is trying to do. You have prevented him from doing that. Once you get that in your mind that these are short bites, you're going to get them every once in a while, but 99% of them, the short bites are your fault. Not the fish's fault. He didn't make a decision to short bite. He made a decision to eat and that's it.

"Here's how you can raise your catchability with jigs–a walleye doesn't sit down there, you go to the bottom, you lift up, and you drop down and 90% of your hits are on the way down. The walleye doesn't sit there and say, Boy I'm going to just bite this jig when it falls down. When you lower your jig and the line goes slack, instead of touching bottom, strike, or, as you lift the jig up with your upward wrist motion and you feel a click or sensation of resistance, strike. When in doubt, strike. It is far better to strike too much than too little.

When using a bottom walker, you don't have it touch bottom as frequently as you would in a river. In the first place, a lake bottom may have soft sediment which will often make the water cloudy. Hence, with lake bottom walkers make the horizontal wire strike the bottom, then raise it up the way you did on the river. Pause 10 or 15 seconds and let the wire strike the bottom again. With any sensation of resistance, then strike. Remember, walleye may give a sharp strike occasionally like a bass, but most of the time, it will be a sense of resistance with a bottom walker. As you gain experience you will be able to qualify the sense of resistance that you feel. If it is a light sensation you will let out more line until the resistance feels stronger. That type of expertise takes a very long time to develop.

"He's trying to bite it on the way up too. With your line there is water resistance, when you are lifting up, you are pulling it away from him. So lots of times that's when a short bite happens. When it falls it is on a slack line, consequently as we talked before, a walleye can open his mouth, flare his gills, and suck in the jig. It's on slack line so it flows into his mouth. Same thing when you are pulling spinners with bottom walkers. In my guide business I can tell you right now I have been out there going through five dozen crawlers trying to teach people how to drop back out, how to work their rod. The guys who just stand there and hold their rod out there all day long, they come up with short bites. The guy that will work his rod and bottom walker will have fewer short bites.

"So work your rod, don't violently jig. People say, 'I don't know how to jig.' Jigging is the easiest thing in the world to do. You put enough weight on to get to the bottom and very gently lift it up a small amount, about four to six inches with a leadhead jig. A blade jig is different. If you should lift it 10 to 12 inches. Lift it up. Drop it down. You feel anything, I don't care what it is, if it is a leaf, a rock, a twig, whatever, you set the hook and keep the line tight. Pretty soon you are going to figure out that that little tick isn't just a rock or a twig; that's a fish. If your jig has been hitting the bottom constantly and then suddenly it does not—strike. Mr. Walleye may have taken it going down. This is one of their favorite ways to take bait fish. It just takes patience and practice, patience and practice. That's all it takes. That's one thing about jig fishing. There are probably more walleyes caught on jigs than any other piece of tackle in the world. It is not expensive; the whole family can do it, and it is very easy to do.

"Then you can go from one type of jig right on to other types, once you get it down. You can lighten your weight up a little bit. You can cast jigs, just like bass fishing. A little grub tail jig with a little half a piece of worm, you can start casting into shore, work your jig out. That all comes with practice. As

I say, put enough weight on to get to the bottom, very gently lift it up, set it back down, lift it up, set it back down. I will tell you right now, again, most of your hits are going to be when they come up, when the line has some slack in it. Don't be scared to tie on some jigs and go do it.

"As we go along through the summer, after the spawn, and out here in the west in my part of the country on the reservoir, they will spawn anywhere from 42 to 50 degrees. It usually comes, depending on the winter, starting in early May up through June and July. Those are your prime months out here. They say why is it the prime month? Well, every minnow in the lake has probably been eaten during the winter, everything spawns in the spring, and there isn't a lot for them to eat. The egg sac fry are not very big after they have spawned. When you get to July and August, then they have a meal to eat, they don't have to scurry around looking for something to eat all the time. The first thing you have to do is to find out where the bait is. Find out what they are feeding on. Do some investigation, whether it is perch, whether it is sculpin, whether it is carp fry. I caught a walleye the other day and put him in the live well, we're talking the first of August. I looked in there 20 minutes later and I'll bet you there were 100 to 200 baby carp fry, about one inch long that he had regurgitated up in the live well. Like I say, they have lots to eat.

"To pull spinners and bottom walkers, it's not a big deal. Out here probably 90% of the fishermen do it. They get their vacation and come, and it's fairly easy to do. The bottom walker was brought into use back in the Missouri River and South Dakota years ago. I can only explain it this way: The darn thing just works too well. That's the best way I can explain it. You tie a three to four foot 12 to 15 pound leader to the bottom walker. Then tie on a spinner rig consisting of five or six fluorescent beads, then a spinner with blades, usually #4, followed by two #2 hooks, spaced three inches apart. You hook the worm right through the head of the crawler, the back hook goes right behind the collar on the worm, which is about a third of the way down. You get your boat up to trolling speed, I usually start about half a mile an hour. Let my line out. I use level wind reels when I troll, they are easier to control your bait on the way down than a spinning reel. Get down to the bottom and then what I do is reel up about two turns, drop my rod back, and if I hit bottom, I lift it right back up. That's where I want to be. I want to be able, with my trolling speed, to lift my rod ahead, drop back, hit bottom. Every time you drop it back you hit, it collapses that spinner a little bit, and allows the walleye to bite.

"You use a sweep set. I don't use a steelhead-bass set where you cross his eyes. You don't have to do that. With the lines we have today, super lines, you hear them all, the braids, the mono. They say mono has a lot of stretch; well it does a little bit, but I'll tell you what when you are only fishing 15 or 20 feet down and just a little ways behind the boat, they say mono has a 25% stretch. I say it is not going to stretch 25% in 50 feet or 30 feet. It might stretch three or four percent. The super-lines like Berkeley Fire Line, yes they don't stretch very much. You get a little better feel of the bottom, and also you can jerk it away from him a little faster because you feel him hit. A lot of times you go along and feel that walleye try to bite it, and you just get up out of your seat, walk to the back of the boat, drop your rod back, and allow that fish to bite. When I first started using super-lines and braids, I lost a lot of fish until I figured out the difference of the two. I still use mono; I use mono a lot. It just depends on the situation that I'm going to be in. It is not something that is very hard.

"Out here in our country we talk "rock". Back east they don't know what "rock" is. Out here we have jagged, big boulders that are not round, sharp volcanic type rocks, some of them as big as a houseboat, four or five feet in diameter. These are perfect places for walleyes to lay in wait for an ambush. They are an ambush fish and that's what they are going to do.

There is a story I like to tell. When you get on a school of fish and they are biting, don't just keep right on trolling down the lake. There is a saying in the tournament game, 'Short drifts cash checks, long drifts take time.' So if you are on some fish and they are biting with spinners or jigs, whatever, turn around, go right back through those fish. Keep working those fish 'til they move, maybe too much boat pressure has spooked them. It does spook them a little bit if you get five or 10 boats fishing in there. Maybe go a little shallower, go a little deeper, maybe you pushed them out. As I said before, get the right attitude. Attitude is you do the thinking; don't let the fish do the thinking for you.

"There are lots of things that enter into this, cold fronts, thunderstorms, you name it. A cold front can be a drop from 90 degrees to 80 degrees. Doesn't sound like much, but that can turn fish off. I watch my barometer a lot. When it falls, a lot of times the day of the fall will be good fishing. Maybe the day or two after that it won't. There is another saying, 'if you get two good days of fishing in, watch out for the third, because it is going to get you.' That's just the way walleye fishing is. It is not hard. It is more like hunting than anything else. I have the same problem as everybody. I have to go everyday and I have to hunt the fish that are biting. That's the main thing you have to do. If you stand there on that spot where you caught them yesterday morning at 10 o'clock and you call your buddy and say 'I'm on these fish and we're going back there, I know right where they are at.' That's when it is going to bite you. You may go back there, they may be there, you may use everything in the tackle box. If they don't feel like biting, they are not going to bite. Don't screw your mind up wondering why. They are not feeding.

"I was on a point up here the other day on Banks Lake, I was on a load of fish. They were scattered all over the lake. I fished them for two hours and I did everything from lead-head jigs to vertical jigging to pulling spinners, but I put a crank on a bottom walker, six-feet of leader, a floating crankbait, a Rapala original (this is a particular type of crankbait). Then I tried a Poe's Cruise minnow. I tried a Smith Wick crankbait. I tried everything very slow to bring it through them. They had already eaten. They didn't feed at all. So I left. I shouldn't have stayed there two hours. I left. I went half a mile away, found some more fish, caught two or three fish right off the bat.

"That goes to show you right there. Fish feed at different times on the lake. Different things affect them. It's not that they say, 'well I'm going to eat here or I'm going to eat there.' It's just that if there is bait there and they want to eat, they are going to eat. We don't want to confuse people with all this gobbledy-goop of big words that nobody understands. Try to understand the fish a little bit.

"Another good suggestion. I started out years ago. *In Fisherman* magazine, a lot of their stuff helped me. *Walleye Insider*, when they came out with that magazine, it's a little tear-out you can buy when you buy an *In Fisherman*. Subscribe to *Walleye Insider*. They have lots of people back there that have been fishing walleyes a long time. They have lots of things on the habitat of the walleye, how he feeds, time of the year, this type of thing. You take the guy who spends a little time to try to understand the walleye. It's not a big deal. I spent a lot of time and I found out that the simpler I can keep it, the better off I am, and enjoy it.

"Don't go out there with the attitude of filling your boat. Catch a couple fish, have a good time, take the kids out, get them started young, get the family back into this thing. We get way too serious on this walleye and all of our fishing. We need to get back to basics on this, any type of fishing. It is not something that is hard. It just takes a little time. I am in the tackle business as well as guiding. I hear it everyday, guys come in and the first thing they want to know, is how deep are they today, what color are they biting on.

"I'll tell you about color. If I were to be sent out and they gave me a rod and reel, some blades, jigs, spinners with #4 blades, bottom walkers, and they said you could choose four colors, which would they be? I'd use hammered brass, hammered silver, chartreuse, and orange. That would be it. At times we become too wild and crazy on colors. You see some of the darnedest things come out and you have to try to separate the myth from advertising.

"I want to get back to this jig deal a little bit. We talked about lead-head jigs, how easy they are to use. I want to take the myth out of how hard it is. The other type of jigging tool we use is, (I think Hedden Sonar came out with it first), it is a little metal body with a little piece of lead on it. It is also known as a blade jig. It has two hooks on it, three holes in the top. You can put your clip in either hole, if you are going to cast it or vertical jig. The middle hole is the best to vertical jig. It is a bait that you have to jig a little higher than most. What it does, it will vibrate up and when you drop it, you jig it up and drop it on a tight line. It is a reaction type bait. A lot of times I have worked a fish right off my bow mount, trying to stay on them, and a lot of times when they are not in a biting mode, they look at that thing fluttering up and down by them, and they will strike at it. I shouldn't say strike at it; they will inhale it. Once you get him on, you have to keep a tight line and get his head turned up. You can lose it pretty easy on these blade baits. They became popular out here in the Columbia about 10 years ago. Two gentlemen from Portland brought them out here from the Midwest. They had been using them back there quite a while. Now there are a lot of guys doing it. In fact in my tournament this year in May, a big fish on the second day was taken on a blade bait right out in front of the dock out here. Everybody thought it was just a river type deal, but it works in lakes, reservoirs, the same way. You just don't have the current to contend with, but you have wind. You can cast it, fan cast it, work it in, lift your rod, let it flutter down, lift it again, let it flutter down. On the Potholes Tournament this year, it worked very well.

"There are lots of different types of lead-head jigs you can cast. Northland makes a whistler jig with a little propeller on it that I really like. It gives a little vibration if you are fishing dirty water. Actually, a walleye feels more with his lateral line than he does sight. They say they can see in the dark. Yeah, they can see in the dark a little bit, but there again I think the vibration of the lure, he senses that, he'll sidle up to it, and then try to strike. In muddy water if you can't see your jig six inches down in the water, I don't think he can see three feet. He is going to feel it. That's why you go to a more vibrating type lure like a whistler jig or a blade bait in dirty water so it will create a little vibration he can feel with his lateral line. A fine line extending along the side of the body, it looks like a little streak and there are thousands of minute hairs there. That's his lateral line. I think he feels more about where bait is with that than with any other thing. That's why when we are out here and we get a wind from the southwest, we always want to fish the muddy side if we can be there in the first half hour. When that mud line starts off a chop bank we get in there and pull spinners, we might go to a bigger five-inch blade on the spinner. We use a quick-change blade-changer so we can change blades, size, and color and go to a little bigger blade in that muddy water. It will cause more vibration. The little fish get disoriented in there; they are swimming around, they don't really know where they are because their lateral line hasn't developed yet, they are small. Walleye go in there and can feel those fish. They say that a walleye, through that lateral line can distinguish types of bait fish. That's something to always remember. If you see that chop start to form, that's when you want to be in there. If you can be the first guy within the first half hour to an hour, sometimes it can be fast and heavy, I'll tell you. If we see the wind come up, we'll fire up, and we may have to run five or 10 miles to a spot, but when we get there, usually we have pretty good luck.

"We back-troll quite a bit, use a drift sock or sea anchor out the front. All that drift sock does is pin that front end down in the wind, and we go backwards. I use it when I am fishing a lot of structure points, where I have to move the boat to stay on contours. Even in flat water I will back troll to pin that front end down, because back trolling you can control your boat a lot faster, stay on contours better, going backwards than you can going forward. It is not very easy to back troll with a steering-wheel boat. I saw a guy do it this year and he was having fair luck at it. It takes a lot of work. But with a tiller boat, with splash guards on the back to keep the water from coming in, it works very well. I would rather back troll. In fact, my Johnson 85 probably has more hours on it back trolling than it does going forward.

"Another thing we want to talk about is your speed. I think a lot of times you start at one speed and you stay at that speed. Say you are trolling spinners, and you are going half a mile an hour. If you're not catching any fish, maybe kick the speed up a little bit. I have gone as high as one and a half to two miles an hour; you have to put good swivels on to do that or it will twist your line. You can't be long-lining your bottom walker. Anytime you are going to be picking the speed up, you have to go to a heavier bouncer. I want my bottom bouncer to be at a 45 degree angle from the side of the boat to the water. Anytime you get your speed up you have to use heavier weight. I have gone as high as three ounces, depending on how high off the bottom the fish are suspended with that three-way and a spinner, bare hook with a leech, or a crawler, and maybe a red bead. A lot of times speed can trigger strikes, so don't forget to change your speed. Don't get stuck in the old rut. If it works today, then it is going to be the same tomorrow.

"As summer goes on anglers say 'Boy the fish are gone, and what happened to them, has everybody caught them?' Well, they are still there; it's just that the bait fish have come alive from the hatch and they have lots to eat. That's when you have to do things a little differently. When the water temperature gets into the 70s in summer, I know a lot of places in the country where they quit fishing. Well, I like to go out. It's a sport to me to see if I'm capable enough to make these fish react to what I am doing. I go to crankbaits. What's a crankbait? Well, I've got a saying, 'It's not a plug; it's a crankbait. It's not a pole; it's a rod. It's not string; it's line.' A crankbait is nothing more than a diving-type plug, where the bill and action determines how deep it will go. They have different actions. They have shad-type baits. They have stick baits, that's a floating type bait, like the Rapala original, the Yakima bait, cruise minnows, a lot of Smith-wicks crankbaits have a shorter bill. They don't have quite as wide a wobble as the Yakima hog boss, Luhr Jensen power dives crankbaits, Hot Lips one-quarter and three-quarter ounce crankbaits, this type of thing.

"The first thing the average fisherman wants to know about crankbaits is the proper way to use them and what crankbait to use. Well, I can understand that. I was very fortunate when I got into this fishing, I had a young gentleman help me years ago to understand crankbaits. What I have done now is just try to improve on that. I look at everybody that is fishing, I see how they are doing it, try to adapt. I learned something this year, a very good friend of mine won a big walleye tournament up at Kettle Falls. He was taking a crankbait that would dive 15 feet, and he was fishing that crankbait in eight, nine, 10, 12 feet of water. Well, it was all weeds in there too. We had some wind that day. If you can get a little wind your boat really won't spook them too much, and all he was doing was short-lining. What I mean by short-lining, he was only running that crankbait about 50 to 60 feet behind the boat, keeping that crankbait up. The more line you put out, the deeper it is going to go. He was pulling that thing with his big motor, three and a half miles an hour. He smacked five fish over 20 inches in about three hours.

"As I've said, I have learned from everybody. I've used the above method out here in this shallower water when I know they are up there feeding on minnows in the weeds. I just want to keep that crank above the weeds. I like to fish with the wind with crankbaits. If I get a foot or two chop, I'll put on a crankbait a lot of times, like a Junior Thunder Stick or a Man's 15, or a Wally Diver. I'll go in there in 10 to 15 feet and I'll short-line over the top of those weeds. I use the seven and a half to eight-foot glass rod; I'm using 20-pound fire line. I still use mono at times, and I keep my drag very loose. I use a glass rod to pull the cranks because I want some shock, like a shock absorber. When he hits that thing, if you're going one direction at two and a half miles an hour, and a six- to seven-pound fish is going the other way, trying to inhale that thing, something has to give. If you use too stiff a rod it will rip it right out of its mouth. The first thing you want to remember when you pull crankbaits is you don't really have to set the hook. To hold pressure on him I lift my rod. If he is a big fish, you are going to feel a huge head shake. If it's a shorter shake it is usually a smaller fish. Those crankbaits take the fight out of them pretty fast. Sure enough, right there at the boat, he made about three dives, we netted him, and the crankbait was still in his mouth. I pulled him up and said, 'Now I'm going to show you why we don't really set the hook when we're pulling crankbaits with a big motor, or whatever you are pulling them with.' It wore a hole three quarters of an inch long where I had him hooked with one hook. One thing you don't want to do is give them any slack at that time because you can net a lot of those fish, and the hooks, crankbait and everything, will fall right out in the net. That's the same as pulling spinners.

One other thing to talk about is cold fronts in summer or spring, and how it affects these fish. Barometric pressure will change and as the pressure falls, it squeezes the air bladder in the fish and stops the bite. If you are on a spinner with bottom walker or crankbaits or whatever, you get a front come through and the next day or two the barometer may remain down. You might keep in mind that usually what happens is they will go to the first drop-off. If you were in 20 feet or 15 feet, and the next major drop-off is 20 to 25 feet or 30 feet, that is probably where they are going to be, and they are going to be bunched up. They are not going to be very active. That is the time I think you should jig-rig, which is just a six- to five-foot leader, or even a four-foot leader, and a bottom walker. Especially if you are fishing over rocks, a little Lindy type lock sinker may work well. If you're not fishing over rocks, maybe it would be best to use a crawler and a red bead. Move real slowly through them, give them time to react, take a little worm blower, blow the tail of the worm up so it will float up just a little bit. Give them time to look at it, don't be running through there too fast. If you work at it, keep the right attitude, you do the thinking, don't let the fish do the thinking for you, if you can scrounge a fish or two out on a day like that, you've had a very good day.

"Getting back to jigs, they may be tougher to use in the wind than spinners and bottom walkers. I really like wind. I like one-foot to two-foot waves, anything to stir things up. I think fishing is better when you get a little wind. I hate 100 degrees and flat water; it makes pretty poor pickings some-times for walleye. If we get a big wind on a big flat, I'll put two drift socks out. Some call them drift socks and others, sea anchors. I put one on the cleat on the front and one on the back of the boat. Then I will use a jig. I will fish in between those two drift socks, the boat will go sideways, and I will drift down through slowly, hopping a jig along, at about a 45 degree angle from the back of the boat. Maybe I'll use a chartreuse twister with a three or four inch little worm grub on it, some-thing like that, a little piece of crawler. Sometimes, you don't have to put anything on there but just a grub. It is a deadly deal at times. As I say, we get too carried away with all this adver-tising and flimflam stuff that people want to run out and buy. Sometimes it is very simple and inexpensive.

"If you're going to buy drift socks, you can buy drift socks from $20 to probably $80, but the ones I use are from Quick Change out of South Dakota. We sell them in our store. They're called Slow-Pokes. One thing about a drift sock is you want to buy one that has a dump line. I see a lot of them out there that don't have a dump line. If you want to pull one of them up full of water, you're going to have to be a pretty stout guy at times. With the dump line, you just pull on the line that hooks on the back of the drift sock, it turns it inside out, and you can pull it up with one finger. If you are going to buy a drift sock, try to buy a quality drift sock. It makes it a lot easier for you. They stow away very easily. I keep them in a bucket in the bow of the boat, hang them up when I come in at night and let them dry out. They dry very fast. Try to fish using that sock as close to the boat as you can. It is just one of those things. Guys say, 'I don't want to fool around with it because of my motor. I have trouble with ropes getting fouled up' I said, 'Well you just drove 250 miles to catch fish, you got a drift sock, and you don't want to use it. Sure it takes a little work, but that's the difference between success and no success. It's very simple.

"The two wind socks are out and the wind has gotten stronger, but the wind socks are keeping us at a reasonable drift speed. Wind socks are seldom used in rivers like the Columbia with strong current. However, there are certain areas where the current is very slow and the river wide, where wind socks are used the same way as in lakes or in impoundments with very slow current.

"At times when I want to follow a contour line and there is no wind, I will hang a wind sock out the bow and follow the contour line with the motor in reverse. This makes control of my boat easier because the bow does not whip around. Other times with wind of moderate velocity when I want to follow a contour line, I will again hang a wind sock off the bow and put the motor in reverse and follow the contour line. Obviously, this will not work in a river with fast current.

"In certain circumstances when there is a light wind, I put out a wind sock from the middle of the boat and again use the motor for control, the same way we did when we had two wind socks out in high wind.

Back trolling with stern into the wind is done frequently with splash guards on the stern. Even with splash guards it can be very wet. With this technique we do not use a wind sock.

A. There is no wind, the boat is back trolling a contour line.

B. In this case the wind is light. The wind sock is slowing the boat by the drag that is produced from the water or the angler can go to E depending if the speed of the wind is high.

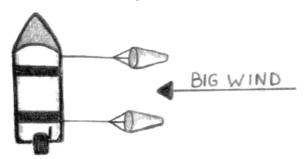

C. Big wind drifting the boat sideways allowing two anglers to fish. The motor is used to push the boat forward or backward for boat control.

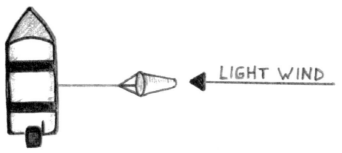

D. One wind sock in light wind, motor against for boat control.

E. Back trolling into wind without a wind sock. When doing this with large waves a splash guard is frequently used to keep water from going over the back of the boat.

As I say, try to keep walleye fishing as simple as you can. There is no magic. You just go out there with the right attitude. Try to talk to some people who are fishing the area. See what they are doing. Always pay attention to the old timers. Give those guys a break. Don't run in on anybody. If you wave to them and talk to them at the dock, they are going to tell you what they are going to do. You can usually tell if a guy is fishing worms, if he's got one leg of his pants all dirty because he has been wiping his hand, or his hat where it adjusts it is all muddy, you pretty much know he is using crawlers or something like that. One thing I do, I don't like all that mess in my boat, so I wash my crawlers. I don't leave them in there for two or three days, but I have a cooler. I take my crawlers, I put them in a bucket, tear up newspaper the longways in strips, get it wet and damp, wash your crawlers, and put them in like a six-pack cooler. Don't drown them, just get that newspaper wet, and when you go out, I use the little cold packs you can freeze, and I put those in there. You reach in there, get a nice clean worm, he's plump, he's nice, and he's cold. You've got to keep your worms cold—not freezing, you can ruin them. There's nothing worse than going out there and having your worms go south on you, right in the middle of the day, you're on a bite and all you've got is a bunch of spaghetti. If you don't wash them, keep them cool with a cold pack.

"Another thing with bait, I go through a lot of bait, because I always keep fresh, good bait on. I don't like to pull that worm for 45 minutes or an hour. I change my bait about every half hour, keeping fresh bait on all the time.

"Go out there and experiment a little bit. We probably ran through that crankbait deal a little too fast. We are going to talk about half ounce crankbaits, which are popular lures out here, a quarter ounce, maybe a Hot Lips crankbait, made by Luhr Jensen. Sure they have 10,000 different colors, but I'll tell you there are about four or five that I use. Yeah, I have all the rest of them in there too, but some of them are just riding around in the boat. All the companies now make a fire tiger, all of them make a Texas shad that is white or a clear-water flash which is kind of a gray, clearwater look, and has a little prism on the inside that flashes. I like that in clearwater, it works very well. They make the crawdad patterns that work well. They make a soft-shell crawdad that works very well. You don't have an arsenal of 500 crankbaits to start, When you have one that you know has been working well for you, then buy four of that particular crankbait for your tackle box. Even then, although you have four, they may not work as well as the first one. I don't know why it's the vibration of it, there is something about it. I've had crankbaits that are supposed to dive 18 feet, a good one will go 20-22 feet. It has the right vibration. I mark that crankbait. The one that doesn't work very well, same brand, same style, same everything—I always give that to my good buddy. I tell him this is a real hot one. Sometimes he comes back and thanks me profusely because it worked so well for him.

"Anyway, talk to other fishermen about crankbaits. There are lots of good fishermen out there. There are lots of good tackle people out there. Try to find a tackle shop where the people know what they are talking about; they're not selling you something just to get it off the rack. I've got stuff that doesn't sell, we thought it would work and it doesn't, so I dispose of it. I try to carry the colors that work. I know I don't carry every color under the rainbow.

Getting back to spinners and bottom walkers, many will tie up their own spinners. I go a step further, I paint my own spinner blades to colors I want. I usually use size #4 or 5 blades. This is something I like to do. Fishermen will tell you they tied the knots, the snells onto these hooks, they're the person who tied them, so they know they're good. If they lose a fish from a snell coming undone, they say, 'well that was my fault.' Nothing worse than being out there, have a nice fish on, and have the snell come untied. Most anglers are learning how to tie their own. They buy the best beads, floats, blades, and hooks and save a lot of money.

"Fishermen agree to disagree. I use VMC straight points, #2s. I feel I get a better hook penetration with the straight point. I have to watch them a lot closer. They'll ding a little easier on the rocks. I got away from using a file to sharpen them and I went back to a stone. I think a file takes too much metal off. That's the main thing. I'll be out here with guys and say "How's your hooks? Are they still sharp?" "Oh, yeah—they're fine." I'll take a look at them and you can see right where they hit a rock and bent over on the end. If you get a nice fish, he is not going to penetrate with a sweep set. Always keep track of your gear, check your mono, check around the leaders, check around the hooks, make sure they aren't frayed. So if you are tying your own, you don't feel too bad about taking it off. Save all those beads and clevises, don't throw your line in the water. I have a little trash bag, I put all my old hooks in there. I stick them in my pocket and when I come in at night I sort the beads and floats back out and use them again. You don't have to throw that stuff overboard. It's just something that makes you feel a little better if you do tie your own combination up and it seems to work, you feel pretty good about yourself that you caught something with what you made.

"I'll talk a little about boats. I use a tiller and I also have a windshield boat too. Almost 90% of your real walleye fishermen around the country are using outboards, not inboards. They can control the boat better with an outboard, save some room. You don't need a $25,000 boat to go walleye fishing. I have some good friends of mine with nice 14 to 16 foot aluminum boats. They put some carpet in the bottom of them to keep them quiet. They don't have GPS units and $600-700 fish finders and this type of thing. They have a basic fish finder. A liquid crystal display (LCD) fish finder is what you want, one that will give you a gray line option on it. What it does when you put it on gray line, it gives you the composition of the bottom from hard to soft. Most of them have directions how to read them. It has a sensitivity which you can turn up or down, and shows you the bottom, shows you how deep they are, how deep you are to the bottom. You don't have to have all that stuff; you can buy all that stuff, and yes, I got 'em. I got GPS units on my boat. It has global positioning capabilities. When I get a bite, instead of throwing a marker over, I use Compu-Troll bottom line. I just switch over to marker, hit that marker, and it gives me a spot. Any time I can turn around and come right back to that spot. I can make that spot a way point, give it a name. What I've found is a rock pile out there in the middle of nowhere sometimes, you can give that a way point, a name, write the name in there, 'Rock Pile Wherever', 'Suzie's Rock Pile', you can name it, and you can drive right to it. Those are all nice, but we didn't have all that stuff years ago, and we still caught a lot of fish. These are just tools that are making it a little easier for you. But you don't need all that stuff.

"If you want to trout fish, bass fish, walleye fish, if you are going to buy a boat, buy a safe boat. Boating safety is #1 with me. Get life jackets and have all the Coast Guard approved stuff. Don't drink and drive on the water. That's another thing that I am dead against; booze and boats don't mix. They mix all right, but they mix the wrong way. I think down the road, I think you are going to see the same thing happening for boats as you do for drivers on the highway.

"If you want a family boat, I have a Lund Tyee that has a windshield. It has bow mounts and depth finders and kicker motors and everything, but it also can be a family boat. Put a little thought into what you buy, maybe talk to different dealers. Go talk to fishermen about the types of boats that they have. There are a lot of good ones out there. I am on the Lund Guide Program. I think they are probably one of the finest aluminum boats made. I like aluminum in this country up here where I can pull it up on shore and I don't have to worry about scratching up the Gelco on a plastic boat. But they're some good walleye plastic boats out there too.

"Put a little thought into it when you go to buy a boat, what kind of fishing you are going to do, and you don't have to spend a lot. There are some good used buys out there; make sure you are getting what you are paying for. I have seen guys buy a boat and the first couple trips out they say, 'I should never have bought this boat for the type of fishing I wanted to do.'

"Another thing we do when it gets into the hotter days is we cast a lot of crankbaits. If we are going to cast up onto a reef, we put the crankbait on. We know the depths it will dive on a retrieve, we will cast crankbaits to weed lines. We'll cast crankbaits to rocky reefs, rocky points. Instead of just going out there trolling a spinner aimlessly up and down the lake and not getting anything, change. I can't emphasize that enough.

If you are going to pull spinners, worms, or other fresh baits, if you are getting them on hammered brass blades one day, they may not want that blade the next day. Put on a chartreuse or a silver or a fire tiger or something like that, but remember change frequently if you are not getting any bites.

If I have two or three people in the boat I'll put something different on every one of them to start, even though they were biting on one thing the day before. I won't change anybody's spinner until one particular spinner and worm have caught two fish. Then, after a period of time, if that spinner loses its effect, I start changing colors again. When you are fishing alone or with one other person, change spinner colors about every half hour. I use a clevis on the spinner shaft that allows you to change blades frequently.

"Another thing to consider is scent. I think if scent does anything, it masks the human scent if you rub it on your hands before working on your spinner or crankbait. I am not sure it does anything when you smear it on spinners or crankbaits. Some swear by the various scents, especially WD-40."

"Gordon, do you ever use slip bobbers? Ed says they don't work well in rivers because of the current and the frequent change in depth."

"Sure I use them, over sunken reefs. We have lots of sunken reefs. You know the depth of the reef so you can adjust the depth that the worm or leech is from the bobber. They work best when the wind is up and there is a chop. This makes the bait go up and down. It is a bit like jigging.

"Walleye fishing can be enjoyed by the whole family. An added plus is they are one of the best fish there are to eat."

SLIP BOBBER SETUP Figure 11-2

Slip bobbers are simple to make. The angler selects the depth he wants his bait to be and slides the bobber stopper to that depth. Large lead shots are placed about 12 to 18 inches above the bait or jig. When ready to cast, the bobber slides down to the split shot. When it lands, the bobber slides up the line and is stopped by the bobber-stopper.

The bobber-stopper can be easily made by using: fly line, Dacron backing (see knot below). It must be tied very tightly to the line.

The bead shown in the drawing is optional. It is meant to keep the slip bobber from going into the bobber.

The bobber-stopper must be small enough to go through the guides and onto the reel so that a normal cast can be made. A proper-sized bobber-stopper knot will stop the bobber when it slides up the line.

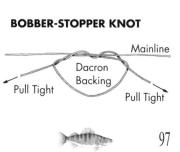

BOBBER-STOPPER KNOT

Mainline

Dacron Backing

Pull Tight

Pull Tight

Chapter XII

TO MAKE
OR NOT TO MAKE
LURES

As previously mentioned, Ed Iman is a professional guide, and I am a trout, salmon, and steelhead fly fishing writer. I enjoy fly tying, plus, being of Scottish descent, I like saving money. A guesstimate is that the average fly costs at most 50 cents to tie. In fly shops, they sell from $1.50 to 2.00. It also gives me a sense of accomplishment when I catch a fish on one of my own flies; especially if it is one I have invented.

By this time, I have been walleye fishing by myself, as well as with Ed. I have learned how expensive it is to buy commercially made jigs and bottom walkers with lead cast into the wire [Illustration of bottom walker - see inside back cover], as well as separate bottom walker weights that can be put on and taken off the wire at will.

This is a comparison of commercial bottom walkers with lead cast in the wire, and those made by an amateur:

Bottom walkers, 0.35 inch stainless wire with 2 ounces of lead weight cast in the wire, unpainted: $1.99.
Same rig, homemade: 54 cents.
Ed feels bottom walker weights do not need to be painted.

Separate detachable bottom walker lead weights, 2 ounces, commercial is 50 cents; amateur 13 cents.

Equipment

The simplest equipment is a 2 ounce lead ladle, approximately $12, and a steel or iron pot, preferable with a round bottom, but a flat-bottomed kitchen pot will do. Do not use an aluminum pot. You will heat the lead satisfactorily but it does strange things to the lead and makes it more difficult to cast. A Coleman gas or propane type stove will work satisfactorily. Do not cast lead in the house. Lead fumes are very toxic. I cast mine in the garage, with the door open. There is very little odor to hot lead vapors. I wear a pair of heavy leather work gloves at all times when casting. The times I have been careless and haven't used the gloves, I have gotten burned.

Before you start making lead weights, read carefully the manual that comes with the lead mold. It does not emphasize strongly enough to keep the mold hot between casting. The technique of heating the lead in a pot, dipping it out in a pre-heated ladle, and then pouring the lead into a preheated mold is difficult. Lead often loses it proper temperature, and you end up with a half-filled mold and a mess on your hands. A better method is the use of the Lead Production Pot ($43.00) (see page 101) is the best for heating lead, and it is the one I use.

Setting up for Casting

1. Collapsible card table with a piece of plywood to protect the surface.
2. Lead Production Pot.
3. Coleman propane or gas camp stove.
4. Molds.
5. Casting lead should be purchased from a tackle store or catalog. Plumbers lead can be substituted. Do not use scrap lead.
6. Kitchen spatula.
7. Thick work gloves.
8. Screwdriver.

Making the Bottom Walker Wire

First you have to make the wire part of the bottom walker. This is very simple. Obtain commercially-made bottom walker and copy it. A standard needle-nose pliers can be used, but a better result will be had using needle-nose pliers with round jaws. Ed uses 0.35 stainless steel wire.

You have now made an L-shaped bottom walker wire.

Casting a Complete Bottom Walker with Weight

The mold is a model BTM-5N, made by Do-It Corporation, Denver, Iowa. All the walleye catalogs carry this, as do most retail stores that carry walleye equipment.

The bottom walker lead mold will have 5 openings, varying in size from 1/2 to 2 ounces. It is only possible to cast one bottom walker weight at a time. Heat your mold on the stove that is next to your casting pot. Then place your previously finished bottom walker wire in the mold so the lead weight will be one-half way down the long wire. Next, hold the mold close to the nipple of your melting pot from which the lead will flow. As

soon as a single mold opening is full, open the mold immediately and—Voila!—you have completed a bottom walker. Don't be surprised if the molten lead continues to dribble after you filled the mold. This is a common problem. I pick up the dribbles of lead with a small kitchen spatula and toss them back into the melting pot. You will be amazed how quickly molten lead solidifies and cools. If the drip becomes excessive, just take a screwdriver and twist the top of the rod that goes into the outlet hole, and the dribble will either stop or slow down. One last thing, a swivel is attached to the end of the wire where the leader goes to the lure.

Bottom walkers with perfectly fixed lead weight work well, as long as you have proper weight for the depth you are fishing, but when you find your bottom walker weight is too heavy or too light, then you must change the whole works, which means untying the line from the reel to the bottom walker and undoing the line from the bottom walker to the lure. This procedure takes time. The answer to the problem is detachable bottom walker weights. We have already discussed the difference between the commercial and amateur costs for detachable bottom walker weights.

To use a separate bottom walking weight, simply slip the bottom walker weight up the wire about half way and put a small kink in the wire to hold the weight in place.

The same mold you use to make the wire with a bottom walker weight, can be altered to make detachable weights. This is done by boring out the part of the mold that the bottom walker goes through. Ed uses a 3/32 drill to do this. Ed then cuts a piece of wire 14 inches long, makes an L-shaped handle at the top leaving straight wire below about 6 inches.

By this time, the molds have been thoroughly heated over the flame of the camp stove. You must have a hot mold at all times. Ed then inserts a wire into the hole of the mold. Next he pours hot lead into the mold opening and instantly pulls the wire out. This is the tricky part. As he pulls it out, he twists the wire vigorously back and forth. He usually hooks the top of the mold onto some stationary object. I use the metal door slide that my overhead garage door runs on.

Occasionally the wire sticks. Then you put the mold over the camp stove and allow it to heat. I have always been able to get the wire free. As you become proficient, you will be able to make these weights quickly. ALWAYS WEAR THOSE HEAVY LEATHER GLOVES AT ALL TIMES.

Jigs

Here Ed Iman and I have had some vigorous discussions. He feels that both painted and unpainted are so cheap, it is really not cost effective to make your own. I started several years ago making lead shad jigs, and I know I do save money on those.

Currently I have two jig molds; one is for blade jigs and one is for round-head jigs. The round-head jig, according to Ed, is the most popular of all for the average fisherman.

Vibrating jigs are used by professional walleye anglers in many competitions exclusively. Ed says this is a jig that is truly cost effective, and suggests I buy a mold and the blanks. Vibrating jigs, complete and painted, are $1.33. To make your own, you need blanks (cost of one: 25 cents) and a mold ($21.99). I guess the cost if you make and paint your own would be about 50 cents.

A mold for round-head jigs is $21. I have been using one. However, as I become proficient at walleye fishing, I will use many varieties of jigs. Unpainted jigs are quite cheap, and I may take up Ed's advice and stop casting jigs. The experts, as well as Ed, find that one jig may work one day and another a different day. Again, as with so much of walleye fishing, it is trial and error. Buying a whole lot of different jig molds is probably not cost effective. I will, however, continue to make my own vibrating jigs.

Spinner Baits

Spinner baits are simple to make and can be made for about 25 to 50 cents. The average walleye shop price is about $2.50 to $3.00. To make your own, just buy a commercial one and copy it.

Crankbaits or plugs

The walleye shop cost is $4 to $6. I listened one night to an expert walleye fisherman who stated that in the course of day, he would lose a dozen crankbaits. Considering the type of crank bait he used, this comes to between $50 and $60 per fishing trip for crankbaits alone. My wife wouldn't let me in the door if I lost $60 worth of crankbaits in one day. As it is, she claims with what I spend on fishing tackle each year, she could buy a mink coat every year. This is obviously a prevarication, but maybe she could buy a fake mink coat.

Cabela's, Janz, and Bass Pro Shops sell unfinished crankbaits. They also sell packs containing 3 to 5 finished crankbaits and supply the hardware which the buyer can attach. This saves about a dollar a crankbait. It is possible to buy unfinished crankbaits and paint them crimson. (I plan to try this next summer.)

Books on Lure-Making

Modern Tackle Craft, C. Boyd Pfeiffer; Lyons & Burford 123
    West 18th Street NY, NY 10011, copyright 1993.
*Lure Making, The Art and Science of Spinner Baits, Buzz
    Baits, Jigs, and other Lead Heads*, A.D. Livingston;
    Ragged Mountain Press, PO Box 220, Camden ME,
    04843, copyright 1994.

Where to Buy Walleye Equipment

Fishermen's Marine Supply - No catalog
1120 N. Hayden Meadows Drive, Suite A
Portland, OR 97217

G I Joe's Inc - No catalog
1140 N. Hayden Meadows Drive
Portland, OR 97217

Cabelas - Catalog
812-13 AV
Sidney NB 69160

Janz - Catalog
Box 89
Maumee, OH 43537

Bass Pro Shops - Catalog
1935 S Campbell
Springfield MO 65898-0123

Additional Sources for Reading

Books

Ed and I have reviewed many books on walleye fishing. The two which we feel are the best are:

Walleye, The Hunting and Fishing Library, 1983, Dick Stranberg.

Walleye Wisdom, Linder, Casanda, Dean, Ripley, Linder, and Stange, Al Linder's Outdoors Inc, 1983.

Magazines

In Fisherman Magazine; Two In Fisherman Drive, Brainard, MN 56401-8097

Walleye In-Sider; Two In-Fisherman Drive, Brainard, MN 56401-8098